# Being Dad

# Being Dad

## Father as a Picture of God's Grace

Scott Leonard Keith

**FOREWORD AND EPILOGUE BY DR. ROD ROSENBLADT**

*An imprint of 1517.the Legacy Project*

*Being Dad: Father as a Picture of God's Grace*

© 2015 Scott Leonard Keith

Published by
NRP Books, an imprint of 1517 The Legacy Project (www.1517legacy.com)
P.O. Box 54032
Irvine, California 92619-4032

Cover design by Quincy Koll.

Printed in the United States of America

---

Library of Congress Cataloging-in-Publication Data is available from the Library of Congress.

Library of Congress Control Number: 2015910191

ISBN: 978-1-945500-39-8 Hardcover
ISBN: 978-1-945500-32-9 Softcover
ISBN: 978-1-945500-40-4 E-book

---

NRP Books is committed to packaging and promoting the finest content for fueling a new Lutheran Reformation. We promote the defense of the Christian Faith, confessional Lutheran theology, vocation and civil courage.

# Abbreviations and Quotations

## Luther's Works

AE    *Luther's Works*. American ed. 55 vols. St. Louis: Concordia and Philadelphia: Fortress, 1955–1986.

WA   D. Martin *Luthers Werke*. Kritische Gesamtausgabe (Weimarer Ausgabe). 73 vols. Weimar, 1883–2009.

## Lutheran Confessional Writings

AC    Augsburg Confession
Ap    Apology of the Augsburg Confession
BC    *The Book of Concord*
LC    Large Catechism
SA    Smalcald Articles
SC    Small Catechism

All quotations from the Lutheran Confessions are taken from, *The Book of Concord: The Confessions of the Evangelical Lutheran Church*, ed. Robert Kolb and Timothy J. Wengert (Minneapolis: Fortress Press, 2000).

## Biblical Quotations and Citations Standards

All Scripture quotations are taken from *English Standard Version Containing the Old and New Testaments*, Wheaton, Ill: Crossway Bibles, 2008.

for

Dr. Rod Rosenbladt

and

Dr. James A. Nestingen

# Contents

# Foreword by Dr. Rod Rosenbladt

Years ago, I offered a series of lectures at the Cathedral of the Advent (Birmingham, AL) on the subject of "fathers." I am one of those lucky few who was given a really great father—a surgeon. Later, I was blessed to be a part of men's groups led by one of the top clinical psychologists of our time: Dr. Paul Fairweather. Paul was professor of pastoral theology at Fuller Theological Seminary. He had done more theoretical work on the place of fathers and children than anyone in his field. And what he bequeathed to all of us men was nothing less than a treasure. So I said in my first lecture that very much of what I had to say was not from seminary training but rather from him (much of it matched my own father and who he was at his core).

Of course, the locus classicus for such a message is in Luke 15: the parable of the prodigal son. As background, I used Helmut Thielicke's *The Waiting Father* (I had not yet discovered Fr. Robert Capon's work on the parables). Thielicke's explication focuses on the surprising, gracious nature of the Father—*not* just on the prodigal's "making himself inwardly homeless" *or* on the subtle danger/plight of the prodigal's "always obedient brother"! He rightly discerns that the parable is centrally about the amazing nature of the Father. (Happily, Thielicke digresses to answer the tiresome charge that the parable is absent in explicit mention of Christ and cross.)

The interest that the lecture series generated was significant enough to warrant a book. So I tasked a former teaching assistant of mine to do that. Scott Keith went on from his bachelor's degree to do doctoral training under the well-known Dr. James Nestingen, formerly of Luther Seminary, St. Paul, Minnesota. Parenthetically, (now Doctor) Keith will doubtless take the place of the late Dr. Lowell Green as *the* Melanchthon scholar of North America. Scott was the ideal pick for this task because (as you will read) his father died very early in Scott's life, and he was always "on the lookout" for ways to fill this immense hole. Studying under me, he says, played some part in that.

We are all painfully aware of the obvious ramifications in today's United States of what a lack of fathers does to a society. And the theoreticians' work backs this up again and again. We may not be very informed about "what a father is" or "what a father does," but we have ample evidence as what the *lack* of a father causes. Dr. Fairweather was out to change that in any way that he could—beginning with the young men in his classes and in his private practice. His training for the PhD in clinical psychology was similar to the training of hundreds of others in his day: Drs. Kohut, Horney et al. But there was very little in that training that had to do with "fathers" and "fathering." And he somehow knew from his own father (a Baptist pastor in the American Baptist Church) that much of the deep healing of individuals had to do with not having been given the fathers whom they (and all of us) really needed—and still need.

Scott will tell you in his introduction that he never intended to write a how-to book. There are more than enough of those—especially in Christian circles. And the quality of these varies from "Okay" to truly awful. The reason for this is that very few authors write out of a "father-defined" childhood. Dr. Fairweather described the voice of the father as "the obscure voice of empathy." If he was right about that (and I think he *was*), our collective tendency, our inner "default," is to discount the father, to "miss" what he is and offers because it is never blatant. We all too easily link "father" with power. Or with hours spent. Or with ball games attended. Or with any of a hundred other things. But nowhere on our collective screens is anything like "the obscure voice of empathy."

Dr. Keith's book is, and will certainly be seen to be, sui generis when compared with other books on the subject. And this will be a reflection of Dr. Fairweather's unique work in the field. In its own way, *his* work was sui generis—so much so that three times he was nominated to be president of the American Psychiatric Association! The aspect of Dr. Keith's book (and Dr. Fairweather's research) that will "stand out" is that the father is called, from the child's earliest days, to function as *analogy*. Those familiar with the work of

Thomas Aquinas will immediately recognize this as his justification of language about God (not "univocal," not "equivocal," but analogical). What Dr. Keith is going to defend is the thesis that fathers are in a unique position to "get across" to a child what Christians call "Gospel"—literally, the *favor dei propter Christum* (favor of God on account of Christ) or "grace." Fathers are, in a thousand different ways, the *only* representative of something other than "law," "rules," "earning" (or *not*), "failure," "guilt," "judgment," "shame," and the rest. *That* is a father's primary calling. Of this, today's secularism knows absolutely *nothing*. And Dr. Keith's book will defend this thesis "twelve ways from Sunday"—and defend it *well*!

Dr. Rod Rosenbladt
Ascension Day, 2015
Concordia University Irvine

# Preface and Acknowledgments

This book is dedicated to Dr. William Rodney Rosenbladt (Rod or Dad Rod), who first introduced me to the pattern-breaking implications of an apologetic from the theology of fatherhood. This he did through lectures, stories, presentations, and his mere presence in my life. He often says that his theology of fatherhood can be traced back to Helmut Thielicke's classic work, *The Waiting Father*, and so this work too will rely on it.

Rod's vocation is that of college professor at Concordia University Irvine, where he has served for more than twenty-five years. There he has taught philosophy, theology, and apologetics. Along the way, he has always gathered around him a group of young men whom he has seen fit to take under his wing. I was lucky enough to be one of those young men.

During my time spent "under his wing," I learned about more than formal theology and philosophy—I learned about being a man and being a father. I had assumed that I knew what it meant to be a man; after all, I was a man. I had assumed that I knew what it meant to be masculine; after all, I had always considered myself to be a masculine man and leader. I had assumed I knew what it meant to be a husband; after all, I was already married. I had assumed I knew what it meant to be a good father; after all, I already had a child. What I came to discover is that there was much that I still needed Dad Rod to teach me.

Learning from Rod turned out to be one of those life events that opened my eyes to things that I had never seen before, helping me to see my role as a man, husband, and father under a completely different light. I had a similar experience when I, at Rod's recommendation, read Robert Bly's work, *Iron John*, and C. S. Lewis's *The*

*Four Loves.* It was as if I had stumbled into a completely unknown world full of men, grace, and a type of love that I, up until that point, had hardly experienced.

What Rod accomplished for me was threefold. First, he taught me that a father's role is primarily that of gracious forgiver and not strong punisher. Second, he taught me that to be masculine did not mean one needed to be big, strong, and rough. Rather, as I learned it from Rod, being masculine meant to be quietly powerful, kind, and gracious. Third, Rod taught me about philia, that non-sexualized love between men that binds them together in a kind of friendship that produces loyalty, respect, and a deep kinship.

The debt this book owes to Dad Rod is obvious and thus is here acknowledged. But just as the sky existed before brave young men learned to fly in it, the idea that a father is a model of God's grace to his children has been an integral part of Reformation theology for centuries. In studying this concept in more detail, I was assisted not only by other authors but also by a number of family members, friends, and colleagues who have been teaching and living these truths in one way or another for years.

To that end, I feel it important to mention just a few of those men. Dr. Jeff Mallinson not only has served as a mentor and good friend but also has been the chief style editor for this work. He is a man worth knowing, a good friend, and a dedicated father. Rev. Paul Koch has provided much of the rhetorical flair for the first few chapters and has donated to the project many fine stories of being a dad. Paul too is a dedicated husband and father of five. Kurt Winrich has been a wonderful conversation partner, as I have frequently forced him to engage me in conversations about fatherhood. Though he often doesn't see it, he is a wonderful friend, mentor, and example of gracious fatherhood. Finally, I am indebted to every person who has submitted a story to this work; without your help, this book would not have been possible.

In the meantime, the place where I have worked and taught, Concordia University Irvine, has provided me the opportunity to practice what I preach here with countless numbers of students. Through my work at the university, I hope that I have been able, in even some small way, to be to those young adults what Rod has been to me. The 1517 Legacy Project has given me the opportunity to pursue further research into this topic, and those involved with 1517Legacy.com have been of the utmost help and encouragement.

Finally, I'd like to say thank you too to all those who know me the best within my particular vocations as husband and father. To my wife, Joy, and my now almost grown children—Caleb, Joshua, and Autumn—as well as to my daughter-in-law, Erika: your place in my life has allowed me to be that which I have always wanted to be: a father. Hopefully I have done it to the glory of God, and I ask too that He forgive me for the times when I have failed, which are many.

Dr. Scott L. Keith
Father's Day, 2015
Concordia University Irvine

CHAPTER 1

# Introduction

## Fatherhood at the Core of the Universe

*An almost perfect relationship with his father was the earthly root of all his wisdom. From his own father, he said, he first learned that Fatherhood must be at the core of the universe [speaking of George MacDonald].*

—C. S. Lewis, *Phantastes*

### The Story

When good fathers die, it's always too soon. I believe that fatherhood is indeed at the core of the universe, yet I never knew my own father. My father died of a rare blood disease when I was two years old, and I have no memories of him. Yet, like every child, I was born listening for the voice of my father, for the voice of his obscure empathy, and I still long to hear my father's voice every day.[1] My mother and grandmother, with the occasional input of an emotionally distant grandfather, raised me. Resultantly, I often have felt as though my entire life has been an attempt to fill the void that being fatherless can leave in a man's heart and psyche. In an attempt to hear my father's voice, I have found many men over the years who have, for a time, filled the void. Replacements included family members, mentors, and friends, but none has been able to fill the void completely.

This void also led me down a path that I could not have predicted or even recognized. For as long as I can remember, I have only desired to do one thing really well: be a father. In turn, I got married very young according to today's standards, and we had children immediately. Before I knew what hit me, I was thrust into what I had always wanted, and yet I did not know what to do. That was in 1995, the same year I began the culmination of my undergraduate studies at Concordia University Irvine. It was there that I first met a somewhat eccentric man, who in many ways would change my life. That man was Dr. Rod Rosenbladt; some of us refer to him as "Dad Rod."

At the time, I was a theology student at Concordia University, and my next three years were full of classes taught by this peculiar theology professor. From his lips, I learned all things religious, theological, philosophical, ethical, and even political. Further, what I noticed was that if I paid close attention, Rod was also teaching me explicitly and implicitly about fatherhood and being a dad. Rod has a knack for teaching his students about grace and graciousness surreptitiously. Thus what I learned from him about being a dad was as much from his actions as from his words.

One of those actions came on a hot summer day in July 1997. During the year, I worked as Rod's teaching assistant (TA), which provided us some supplementary income to buy groceries, diapers, and the like. Receiving no TA money during the summer meant that, for us, summer in Southern California was no fun at all, just hot and depressing. But on that day in July, I got a call from Rod asking me to come over to bring my wife, Joy, and our two small boys so that they could go for a swim. When we showed up at his house, he politely pointed Joy and the boys toward the pool and told them to have fun. I stayed behind to talk with Dad Rod. We drank coffee, talked about what we were both working on, and basically shot the breeze for about an hour. When he somehow sensed that Joy and the boys were on their way back, he quietly slipped upstairs for a few minutes. When he came down, he had an envelope in his hand and gave it to me, simply saying, "I know summers are hard for you." I didn't even look in the envelope; as tears welled in my eyes, I just hugged him and thanked him. Soon after, Joy and the boys arrived back at the house, and we all said our good-byes and headed to the car and back to the university. When we got home, I looked in the envelope and found five crisp $100 bills. That gift and his grace changed our world that summer. Dad Rod had stepped in when all seemed lost to us and made things, at least for the moment, OK.

There are many more stories that I, and several others, could tell of Rod that would illustrate his graciousness. Some will be told later in this book. But the point is not to elaborate on Rod's graciousness specifically; rather, the point is to demonstrate what the shadow teaches that Dad Rod casts. Primarily what it taught me and what I came to understand is that being a good dad means modeling to my children the same grace and graciousness that Dad Rod has shown me in his every step as a professor, mentor, and friend. By listening closely to Rod's words and watching his quiet actions, I learned—and learn to this day—many things about being a dad. Rod taught me that when things are basically good between a father and his children, almost everything else in a child's life would be basically good too. I learned that when there is no battle to be fought between a father and his children, the children receive a wonderful, freeing gift. A good dad's children receive the gift of grace, peace, and freedom.

## The Problem

Though it seems clear that, like me, every child feels the deep need for a father, sadly, according to U.S. Census Bureau data, 43 percent of all children in the United States live in a home where there is no father.[2] The social ramifications of this dismal reality are staggering. According to the U.S. Department of Health, 63 percent of all youth suicides occur in fatherless homes.[3] The same agency reports that 90 percent of all runaway children live in a home where there is no father. Further, the Centers for Disease Control and Prevention reported in 2012 that 85 percent of children who show behavior disorders come from fatherless homes, twenty times the national average.[4] A staggering 80 percent of convicted rapists come from fatherless homes.[5] And lastly, children raised in homes without a present father, either due to being born out of wedlock or as the result of divorce, are more than twice as likely to drop out of high school before completion.[6]

This crisis even extends into the life of faith and the health and wellness of the Church. In 1994, the Swiss carried out a landmark study that revealed the truth about the faith lives of children. The study found that it is the religious practice of the father of the family that, above all, determines children's future church attendance or absence.[7] Not surprisingly, the study revealed that if both parents attend church regularly, 33 percent of their adult children will also attend regularly. It is also no surprise that if only one parent—the mother—attends regularly (and the father is a no-show), a mere 2 percent of adult children will attend regularly. The unexpected result was that if the father alone attends (and the mother is the no-show), 44 percent of adult children become regular attendees.[8]

In short, if a father is not a regular church attendee, the children will most likely not be church attendees as adults, no matter the faith practices of the mother. If a father practices his faith regularly, regardless of the practice of the mother, 60 to 75 percent of his children will practice his faith as adults. Even a father's irregular faith input and practice will result in more than half of his offspring coming to, staying in, and practicing the faith as adults. In short, fathers matter a great deal when it comes to the faith of their children. In fact, it could be argued that nothing in a child's faith development matters more than the picture of faith that they see in their own father.

## Disclaimer

I am not proposing to attempt this from a psychological perspective. I am not a clinical or any other type of psychologist, nor do I claim to have any expertise in that field. I am a husband, parent, associate dean, college professor, theologian, and student of the Reformation who is interested in the intersection between the theology of the Reformation and the apologetic goodness in a father's love. My disclaimer is that, as a theologian, I defer to the professionals in the field of psychology and sociology. But at the same time, I am a father. I am a father who has, over the course of the last twenty years, considered these questions in great detail from a theological perspective. Further, I think that a response is needed to our culture's attack on men generally and fathers specifically. According to the U.S. Census Bureau, twenty-four million children in America—one out of every three—live in biological father-absent homes. We need men to be good fathers, not just sperm donors. Our society needs it, the Church needs it, and our children most certainly need it.

## A Theological Solution

I think that what is needed is a theological solution. The essential Christian claim is that God was in Christ reconciling the world unto Himself.[9] A Christian father approaches this claim as true. That is, he approaches the Gospel message as true and powerful. The Gospel is the message of hope on account of Christ. Ours is the God who acts graciously toward us on account of Christ, even when we openly reject He who deigns to save us. This is as Paul also writes: "But God shows his love for us in that while we were still sinners, Christ died for us."[10] To understand the Gospel is to understand that the Word of Christ has power. This is the Word of forgiveness and of life. It is the Word of freedom and a declaration of adoption. It is the power of God unto salvation for all those who believe.[11] It brings faith and renewal. When proclaimed, the Gospel has the power that nothing else on this earth does; the Gospel literally brings us dead sinners to life. This Word of salvation and vivification comes to us, always, on the lips of another. We literally hear and experience the Gospel in the relationships we have with one another.

Now if this is true, we should expect to see shadows of this truth in the earthly realm that is our world. We should expect these shadows in the people who are closest to us and love us the most. We live in a world and culture wherein we do not often recognize the shadows of God's truth all around us. Furthermore, when we do recognize them, we lack the ability to fully comprehend or explain them. We struggle with an inability to express God's greatness. The great Christian thinker Thomas Aquinas taught that the shadows of God's goodness are all around us. That is, we see things that remind us of or point us to God and then use analogy to explain them. In this sense, good fathers are a reflection of God's grace. And even though a good father's goodness is not the same as God's goodness, it is, in a way, like it. A father's love is not the same as God's love, but it does reflect the truth of God's love. God shows us a glimpse of Himself when He grants us the gift of a good earthly father. We then point to something or someone here in our everyday life, our dad, and say God is like that.

God has also promised to meet us in His Word, in His sacraments, and in the communion and mutual consolation and conversation of His saints.[12] This is the concept that we receive forgiveness from those that God has called into our lives. The picture of a good father is the picture of consolation that He provides in the home to point His children toward Christ. The good father is the penultimate mutual consolation of the saints, so noteworthy that God has intended it to occur in the most intimate setting, the home, from the earliest of ages. This book will not be complete in its treatment of possible topics, statistical details, psychological or sociological analysis, or even biblical theology. This book, if it does what I intend, will draw a picture of a good father given as a gift by a good God in order to bring children, to bring little sinners, to Himself. This is why it is so utterly important for fathers to be to their children the carriers of the Word of life.

## This Is Gospel, Not Law

The approach taken will be one of analogy. I will use the parable of the prodigal son as a jumping-off point. As the Lutheran theologian Helmut Thielicke once said, this parable shows us that the Father is the "heart of all things."[13] The beauty of this parable is that we can so easily relate to it. We can see ourselves as either the hateful younger son or the petulant self-righteous older son. Furthermore, we all long for, or to be, the father who is all forgiving in the face of absolute loathing. This parable provides a picture or pictured story of what the Father's love is like. My task will be to awaken in men the feeling that they are this same-pictured story, in an admittedly smaller way, to their own children.

Yet in order to do this I will need to present a solution to the "fatherhood problem" that is based in the Gospel and not the Law. In other words, I will not take the same old tired approach of telling you that you need to "train" your children right. You will instead hear stories, pieces of wisdom, and verbal pictures of the power that is ever present in the forgiveness of the Gospel, especially when it comes on the lips of a father.

The Law will never produce righteousness or lead to salvation. The Law always accuses. Our sin is what causes us to believe that the solution to every problem, or any problem, is to throw just a little more law at it. What we fail to realize is how natural the Law is to us. Gustaf Wingren said this well when he claimed, "The Gospel always breaks into a world that has already got law, and for which law is not news, not a novelty."[14] It is the Gospel that goes against the norm. It is the Gospel that is a novelty. It is the Gospel that is not only "news," as Wingren says, but "Good News." As Martin Luther so eloquently phrased the paradox of the Gospel in his great Galatians commentary, "The Gospel supplies the world with the salvation of Jesus Christ, peace of conscience, and every blessing. Just for that the world abhors the Gospel."[15]

The parable of the prodigal son is as powerful as it is because it is a word of forgiveness spoken into a world rightly expecting law. Just when we think condemnation is what is needed, the father steps in and hands out only forgiveness. This is the picture of the father that Christ paints, and this is the shadow of "fatherness" for which this book will advocate. If fathers are to make a substantive and powerful impact in the lives of their children, it will be by fulfilling the roles that God said they will: as little Christs and forgivers of their own children. If there is a "father problem" in our society, and I think there is, the solution is more Gospel, more forgiveness, more fathered graciousness, not more rules.

## Let's Get It Right

The goal is to give a gift to the reader of a picture of a good father. In the end, connections will be made between good earthly fathers and the picture of God as our true Father. This book will never be a how-to manual. Many specifics will be left out. I am approaching this work through the narrow lens of how good dads who forgive point to the truth of a good God who forgives. There will be no ten steps to better disciplined children here. As I have said, I believe that the law is natural to us and we need very few tips regarding its implementation in the home. If we choose to be overly permissive, that is not the Law but rather our own sin. If we choose to be rigidly legalistic in our approach to fatherhood, that is allowing the character of the Law to rule over our household in place of the Gospel. But if we forgive sins, we cast a reflection that points to a God who forgives in Christ. It is in this way that we understand that fatherhood truly must be at the core of the universe.

## CHAPTER 2

# Two Lost and Found Sons and the Dad in the Middle

*If we allow ourselves to be kindled by the love of the Father's heart and then this very day look around for those to whom we can apply this love . . . only if we enter into this living circuit of divine love and let it warm us and flow through us will it suddenly become clear to us what it means and what a joy it is to know the fatherly heart in heaven and the blessed brotherly heart of our Lord and Savior.*

—Helmut Thielicke, *The Waiting Father*

## An Older Tale

The storytellers of our day—those crafters of our shared narrative—have shaped for us a troubling story. From the nightly news, to the captivating humor of our sitcoms, to the thrill of Hollywood blockbusters, we hear a story that not only promotes but celebrates madness, and this madness can be infectious. This becomes clearer every day as we see fathers and the concept of the father denigrated in popular media. The insanity lies in putting forward the idea to everyone that watches and hears that we don't need a father when, in fact, we need a father like we need our next breath. This negative portrayal of the father is not just sin; this is a form of insanity that is so pervasive in our culture that it has reached terrifying heights. To be clear, we know deeply and personally that we did not all have good fathers, or even any father for that matter. But these unfortunate life circumstances should not imply that we do not need a father. We needed a father from the start. In fact we were born longing for the sound of a father's voice to guide us. We were born needing to hear and feel his love and grace.[1]

But there is a much older story than these modern tales, a story that has functioned as an escape and barrier from such insanity, a story that paints a vastly different picture than that of the bungling father who provides little more than a financial support and comic relief. It is a story that has been handed down from generation to generation and perhaps has never been so needed as it is today. It is a story that was first heard from the lips of Jesus Christ. Christ was the ultimate storyteller. He told stories throughout His three-year ministry to deepen the meaning of His teachings, sometimes to confound His listeners, and often as metaphors meant to paint a picture of the Kingdom of God.

As Christians we believe that the Gospel is true and that we have a Father that sent His own Son so that we could be His children; this framework necessarily affects both our view of human fatherhood and also our perspective on the fatherhood of God. This biblical imagery conveys a picture of a father who doesn't operate according to payment plans. He gives freely. Likewise, human fathers have the unique vocation of modeling the love of the Heavenly Father in their own homes. They are called to give freely without expecting anything in return, even when they are the offended party. Throughout the pages of the New Testament, we find some forty-six fatherhood stories told by Christ, but one stands out especially today. It is the story of a father and his unmerited forgiveness toward his sons,[2] and it has been underappreciated for too long. It is the picture Christ gives us of the idealized father-son relationship. This is the model we will use to develop our tale of being a dad. Our hearts are kindled by hearing the story of the father's love.

## The Parable of the Prodigal Son

*Luke 15:11–32*

And he said, "There was a man who had two sons. And the younger of them said to his father, 'Father, give me the share of property that is coming to me.' And he divided his property between them. Not many days later, the younger son gathered all he had and took a journey into a far country, and there he squandered his property in reckless living. And when he had spent everything, a severe famine arose in that country, and he began to be in need. So he went and hired himself out to one of the citizens of that country, who sent him into his fields to feed pigs. And he was longing to be fed with the pods that the pigs ate, and no one gave him anything.

"But when he came to himself, he said, 'How many of my father's hired servants have more than enough bread, but I perish here with hunger! I will arise and go to my father, and I will say to him, "Father, I have sinned against heaven and before you. I am no longer worthy to be called your son. Treat me as one of your hired servants."' And he arose and came to his father. But while he was still a long way off, his father saw him and felt compassion, and ran and embraced him and kissed him. And the son said to him, 'Father, I have sinned against heaven and before you. I am no longer worthy to be called your son.' But the father said to his servants, 'Bring quickly the best robe, and put it on him, and put a ring on his hand, and shoes on his feet. And bring the fattened calf and kill it, and let us eat and celebrate. For this my son was dead, and is alive again; he was lost, and is found.' And they began to celebrate.

"Now his older son was in the field, and as he came and drew near to the house, he heard music and dancing. And he called one of the servants and asked what these things meant. And he said to him, 'Your brother has come, and your father has killed the fattened calf, because he has received him back safe and sound.' But he was angry and refused to go in. His father came out and entreated him, but he answered his father, 'Look, these many years I have served

> you, and I never disobeyed your command, yet you never gave me a young goat, that I might celebrate with my friends. But when this son of yours came, who has devoured your property with prostitutes, you killed the fattened calf for him!' And he said to him, 'Son, you are always with me, and all that is mine is yours. It was fitting to celebrate and be glad, for this your brother was dead, and is alive; he was lost, and is found.'"

## The Departure

We are told that, once upon a time, there was a man who had two sons. These sons were as different as can be: the older one obedient and prideful and the younger reckless and ungrateful. Their story, as it unfolds, illustrates our own struggles and tensions, and it is easy to find that we are reflected in these sons. Now, their story is undoubtedly one of treachery, betrayal, and resentment, but standing right in the middle, in a surprising and comforting way, is a dad, a dad who demonstrated a powerful and unflinching love.

The story begins not with a peaceful scene from a Monet painting but with the shouts of the younger son making demands of his father. This ungrateful child demands from his father his share of the inheritance so he can get on with life on his own terms. This may seem strange to us today, since we know inheritance usually comes after the death of the benefactor, but this younger son would not wait. This was tantamount to shouting, "I wish you were dead. The only thing of value that I see in you is your money, so give it to me!" If you are a father, you have likely felt the scorn of your children, and you know how much it hurts. Children's disrespect for a father is painful. This act on the part of the younger son is the ultimate act of disrespect toward his father. The son is literally asking his father to commit suicide.[3] Nonetheless, the father acquiesces to the son's impetuous demands and divides what he has and gives half of everything he is and everything he has to the younger son. The son then doubles down on his disrespect toward the father and quits the family, leaving his father's home in order to head to a far-off country. He makes a clean break, abandoning the security and identity found in his father's home.

This son has a great time for a while, but he burns through his father's gift in no time, consuming his inheritance with useless debauchery. But we are told that in this far-off country, a famine ravages the land, and the lost son ends up in a state of deep need. He is without a home and becomes a wanderer in a strange land. He is hungry and desires to be fed. This wayward son has neither the drive nor the earthly possessions to keep him going; his vanity now gone, he is empty. In his dire straits, there remains for him no comfort for his soul and no healing balm for his affliction. I have seen this type of hopelessness in the eyes of many young people, and it often leads to a deep despair and sometimes even to self-destruction. As the story is told, this is the exact precipice upon which this younger son now teeters.

Realizing that he is in deep need of help, the younger son attaches himself to a kindly stranger that he discovers is a pig farmer. In the traditions of his father's household, herding pigs and working with unclean swine is unthinkable and represents great desperation. It is utter shame as well as the final crushing of the young son's pride. With all his pride gone and all his vanity stolen by his wayward living, this young son has nothing left to rely on but guilt, shame, and desperation. Yet if that were not enough, one act of degradation remains: the younger son is so hungry that he is tempted to eat the garbage with which the pigs are fed. He once was a son of a powerful, wealthy, and gracious father; now he is no more than an orphan and servant fit only to eat with the pigs.

Obviously, this son is not acting like the son of a gracious and loving father; rather, he is acting as though he was no son at all. He is not of his right mind. He is insane. To deny his father is an act of insanity. Insanity is often diagnosed when people perceive what is unreal as real or reality as a sham or when they don't perceive reality at all. This is not the entirety of the doctrine of sin, but the son's rebellion reminds us of the Apostle Paul's words: "Therefore God gave them up in the lusts of their hearts to impurity, to the dishonoring of their bodies among themselves, because they exchanged the truth about God for a lie."[4] Truth is seen as lies, and lies are viewed as though they were true. The lie had become truth to the younger son, and suddenly the truth in a moment of clarity occurs to him.

## The Return

Finally, the reality sets in, and this broken son realizes that as a mere servant, as a slave in the home of the man he wished dead, he would have more food than he could ever eat. The son realizes that his only chance for life is to return to his father, make a confession of his sin, and plead for even a mere semblance of the father's mercy. He seems to still have a remembrance of a father's mercy, a knowledge that was within the younger son the entire time but clouded by his ambition, envy, lust, shame, vanity, and hatred. The son realizes that his only hope is to give up all claims of righteousness before his father.

The lost son knows that he has no hope of being received by the father because there is nothing good in him and there never has been. He has hit rock bottom and is even willing to give up any right of sonship before the father, yet when he returns, something inside him beckons so that he still calls him "father." The young son sets his mind to dare to ask that he be taken back and placed in the lowest position in his father's house: a slave. How could he think that his father would take him back after the many filial crimes he committed against his father? He somehow remembers his father's graciousness. He decides to try to cut a deal with is father. Welling up from deep inside him bubbles memories of his father's goodness, even toward servants and slaves. He still has a certain confidence that even in the face of his great sin, his father will reach down inside himself and find grace. His father will do what fathers do: make the impossible possible for him.

So the son sets off to return. But little does he know that his father has been longing for his return the whole time, never giving up hope that he might return. He stands out on a large balcony with a clear view of the walkway up to the home continually scanning for his beloved son's arrival. He is not looking for the return of a slave or a servant; he desires the return of his son. And then he sees what his aching heart longs to see; the father sees his son far off in the distance. His heart swells with compassion toward his son and joy at his unlikely return. The father leaps from his perch with a frenzy of emphatic energy and runs down to embrace his son, nearly knocking him over as he embraces him. The father literally falls upon his son's neck and covers his face with kisses. The son is pardoned, set free, forgiven, released of guilt, and accepted into the family once more, and he has had his shame taken away before he even gets to utter a word. His weak, pathetic, misguided, and useless confession, which he spent so much time practicing, isn't even needed or wanted. His deal is not wanted—not wanted because the dead need not confess, they only need to be brought back to life. It is as the Episcopal theologian Fr. Robert Capon notes: "Confession is not a transaction, not a negotiation in order to secure forgiveness; it is the after-the-last gasp of a corpse that finally can afford to admit it's dead and accept resurrection."[5]

Seeing the father's joy produces even more guilt in the son. It is obvious that the son need not confess; the father lets him begin his confession anyway. So says the son, "Father, I have sinned against heaven and before you. I am no longer worthy to be called your son."[6] Immediately, before he can even finish his mea culpa, the father cuts him off. Here the story slows down for just a moment in order to present one of the kindest, gentlest, and most tender pictures painted in any story we have ever heard. The father spares the son, the chief of sinners, the indignity of his full confession. The father in his grace wants nothing to do with his unnecessary words. The father wants his son back now, no time wasted. This sinner's justification is at hand. The son's pardon and adoption are all wrapped into three sentences by the father: "Bring quickly the best robe, and put it on him, and put a ring on his hand, and shoes on his feet. And bring the fattened calf and kill it, and let us eat and celebrate. For this my son was dead, and is alive again; he was lost, and is found."[7] And they celebrate the son's joyous return.

It is worth taking a closer look at these actions of acceptance and adoption. First, the lost son is quickly covered in the robe of the father's righteousness, dressed in the garment of salvation. We can easily see the imagery of Isaiah: "I will greatly rejoice in the LORD; my soul shall exult in my God, for he has clothed me with the garments of salvation; he has covered me with the robe of righteousness, as a bridegroom decks himself like a priest with a beautiful headdress, and as a bride adorns herself with her jewels."[8] The robe that is placed on the son represents his complete and utter forgiveness. He is now so covered by the father that a casual passerby might confuse the two. He brings nothing; he need not bring anything to the father, not even his confession. He is literally covered in the father's forgiveness.

The signet ring of sonship is placed on the son's finger, giving him authority to buy and sell on the father's behalf. Placing the ring on his finger is the ultimate act and sign of trust given by the father back to his lost son. This signet ring could in our day be called a signature ring. This is the ring used to make an indention on the wax seal that would literally "seal" a contract. With this ring, the wayward and fornicating son could yet one more time sell what belongs to his father and squander his riches with prostitutes. He did not earn this trust; he could not earn it, as he is the one that originally destroyed it. Yet in his love and graciousness, the father insists that the son possess it regardless of his lack of trustworthiness. He who cannot be trusted is given trust, just as we who cannot believe are given our faith.

The father demands that his servants place shoes on his son's feet. Shoes would indicate to the outside world, and to those in the father's home, that the lost son who has returned is truly a son and not a slave. Finally, the father demands that the best and fattest calf be butchered and cooked so that they could have a party. At the party there is music and dancing and great joy. The astounding reason for this revelry is that a dead son was brought back to life. Let us all make merry! When a dead person comes to life, a party of this caliber, which has not previously been seen, is obviously required.

## Green with Envy

But our story is not finished. Remember, this is a story of a man who had two sons. There is another son, the older son, and he is lost too; he's simply lost in plain sight. Yet the older son is not lost in obvious sin—he is lost in sanctimony and self-righteousness. He is busy in his work—the self-righteous are always great workers—so busy that he doesn't even initially notice his brother's return. He eventually hears the noise from the party. He has been working hard in the field as he did before his brother's departure and during his long absence. As he approaches the house after a long day at work, he hears music and dancing and asks a young boy what is happening. The boy seems thrilled to tell the older brother the good news that his father is throwing a magnificent party because his lost brother has returned. Children are always overjoyed to share the good news.

At once, the older brother becomes consumed with anger and righteous indignation. He is so angry that he cannot bring himself to join in with his father and refuses to enter the house. Suddenly, the father appears beside him (someone must have run in and tattled on the older son—perhaps the young boy; children love to tattle too), entreating his older son to come in and join the party. This older son obviously deserves to be scolded for his arrogance and defiance of the father. Yet the father, as he is apt to do, shows grace and bids the son to join him in his happiness.

Now here we see the blindness, perversity, selfishness, and vanity of the older son who has all this time set himself up to be seen as the "good son." Overcome with pride, he fires kill shots at his father with both barrels. "Look, these many years I have served you, and I never disobeyed your command, yet you never gave me a young goat, that I might celebrate with my friends."[9] Finally, the older son fires the final death shot at his father. He explains his father's real error: never realizing how much better he was than his younger brother. "But when this son of yours came, who has devoured your property with prostitutes, you killed the fattened calf for him!"[10] He blames the father for all his misery. He blames his father for treating a wayward dead son better than the one who has been in front of him all the time. The son makes vicious cuts at the father for never realizing what he had right in front of him.

At this point, it seems sure that we will finally see the end of the father's graciousness and patience with his sons. After all, wouldn't he be justified in turning with anger toward his older son and unleashing all his pent up frustration on him? The father should have then and there renounced his son's wicked words and his wicked heart and used his right as a father to revoke his son's inheritance. Yet what he does instead is apply just enough Law, followed with a reminder that this is about the good news (Gospel) of redemption and resurrection. The son cannot accept the father's forgiveness because he believes his hard work is keeping him alive. Remember, only the dead can be brought back to life. So the father must first kill his sanctimony and allegiance to a false law. Firmly and surely, he says, "Son, you are always with me, and all that is mine is yours. It was fitting to celebrate and be glad, for this your brother was dead, and is alive; he was lost, and is found." The father asks why his older son cannot understand this. He tells his son, "You are the owner of this house." The father wants his son go in, enjoy the party, and be dead to his pointless rules about how all these things should be enjoyed.[11] It is as if he says to his son, "So do yourself and everybody else a favor: drop dead. Shut up, forget about your stupid life, go inside, and pour yourself a drink."[12] His fatherness is revealed in his willingness to set the impetuous son free to be dead as well. Only in the son's death can the father's grace, forgiveness, and resurrecting power truly be shown. The father as the model of grace only works because the father knows his children's weakness. The father is not permissive; he forgives, saves, and sets free!

## Lost and Found

Of course, this classic story is best known to us as the parable of the prodigal son, though perhaps we might better call it "The Two Lost and Found Sons and the Dad in the Middle." As Jesus tells this parable, He brings us to the realization that we are both the prodigal and the self-righteous son in need of an utterly loving and gracious father. In the sons' actions, we see how we approach God, our Father, bringing nothing of merit. We somehow know that even in the face of our great sin, God will make the impossible possible for us and be gracious toward us. Fathers, including the father in this story, are shadows of that innate reality that lies within us. The picture of the father as good and gracious lies within us all, and this story shows it to be an accurate picture.

Of course, we recognize that there is no atonement, no sacrifice in this story; that is, there is no sacrifice of Christ to pay for the sin of the younger or older son. Some will ask, Where is Christ in this story? Christ is in the party and in the death of the fatted calf. The calf killed for the celebration is actually the Christ figure in the parable. Again, Capon is helpful on this point, as he asks us to consider what a "fatted calf" actually does. Says Capon, "It stands around in its stall with one purpose in life: to drop dead at a moment's notice in order that people can have a party. If that doesn't sound like a lamb slain from the foundation of the world—who dies in Jesus and in all our deaths and who comes finally to the Supper of the Lamb as the pièce de résistance of his own wedding party—I don't know what does. The fatted calf proclaims that the party is what the father's house is all about."[13]

We need to recall that it is Jesus who tells the story in the first place. This is the same Jesus who says of Himself, "I am the way, the truth, and the life, no one come to the Father but by me,"[14] and "I and the Father are one."[15] Jesus is clearly He who grants us access to the Father. So it is not just anybody telling this story—it is Jesus Christ Himself, who is our atonement. Jesus and the Father are one; He is in the Father and the Father is in Him. He is not imagining a picture of an assumed heaven that is open to prodigals like you and me; in Him, because of Him, His home is actually open to us. The storyteller tells us a story that happened in His own house, a house to which we gain access on account of His life, death, and resurrection. We should not forget that when we read this parable.

This one parable can have an astounding, miraculous effect on those who are lost in unbelief. This parable is a story, and like all good stories it tends to resonate with us on a level that we cannot even describe or comprehend. Many who read this story have had great fathers, some have had bad fathers, and others have had no father at all. Nonetheless, this story remains one of the ultimate analogies of love and caring that has ever been presented. The miraculous nature of this tale can be seen most clearly when it is told to those who are not at all familiar with the Bible. Why? This is a powerful story because it touches a need that lies deep within all of us: unconditional fatherly love.

The love of a father is deep magic that can be sensed by readers both Christian and non-Christian. The grace of an earthly father is a mere shadow or foggy picture of the grace of our Father in heaven. This story feels true because it is true. This tale tells everyone that the father's love for his children, for us all, exists even though he is fully aware of all that we have done. This isn't the story of a doting grandfather who doesn't really know the details of the situation and just steps in with a smile saying, "I'm sure it will all work out in the end." We know that without the father stepping in and fixing it, it won't work out in the end. This is the story of a father and his sons. The father knows of both our greed and our licentiousness. The father knows of our pride and sanctimony. The father knows of our deep despair, our mistrust of him, and our hopelessness apart from him. Yet the father loves us and shows us mercy, and in this tale, Christ tells us precisely that.

## Our Story

This parable represents our story, our personal fairy tale, and it stands in stark contrast to the story being told in our daily consumption of news and entertainment. The Father has shown us pure love and affection, and we have flat out denied Him, forsaken Him, and wished Him dead. This is the true situation for us all. Think of Romans: "For as by the one man's disobedience the many were made sinners."[16] We are the disobedient sinners, and as a result, death and condemnation is what we deserve. Our world apart from His unmerited salvation is utterly hopeless. Yet the Father offers life through His Son. The white knight that is from a far-off land rides in to save the day. Our innate knowledge that we are both the prodigal and the older son, connected to this story of a loving father's response, joins all of us in a very powerful way to the true tale of God our Father.

In this book, I want to cast a spell on you. You will read some Scripture, you will hear stories from fathers and sons, and you may even glean some wisdom. But most of all, what I hope to accomplish with this book is to help you experience some of the good magic that is a father's love and what it does for all of us. I do this with the desire that you might learn to share the love of a father with your children and maybe even with a few others who are not of your own blood. Remember, our story is the tale of two lost and found sons and the dad that has been in the middle the whole time. Our tale is the tale of the Father who loves us and sent His Son, that through His death and resurrection we might be like one who "was dead, and is alive" in order that we might be claimed as His own child. Our calling and our vocation are to share our tale with others, starting with being a dad to our own children.

# CHAPTER 3

# The Lost Art of Masculinity

## The Need for Masculine Fathers

*Upon the death of King David to his son Solomon:*
*"I am about to go the way of all the earth," he said.*
*"So be strong, act like a man!"*

—1 Kings 2:2

### A King's Heart

Some men can transform a room simply by walking through the door. These men bring with them something ineffable yet discernible. The truth is, in our world, there aren't many of this type of man left. Have you ever met a man who had this quality? If you had, you'd remember him. Just what is it about this type of man that can cause such an effect simply by entering a room? The answer may very well be something we already know but are afraid to praise publicly. Instead, we politely decline to answer, yet still we know the answer— it's masculinity. In this chapter, I will define masculinity as a male's quiet confidence and strength of character that finds expression in graciousness. Despite what our current cultural milieu would tell us, masculinity is a laudable trait. Of course, you wouldn't know it by watching television, going to the movies, or engaging contemporary culture or modern media. It seems that instead of being portrayed as masculine, almost every male character portrayed in modern media is impotent, stupid, incapable, or irrelevant.

As I observe our situation, I think most men live in a world of desperation. Men are desperate to hear that it is OK to be a man. Desperation leads the modern man down dark paths. But the life of a man does not need to be this way. Masculinity is a good gift given to men by God for a purpose. Truly masculine men are embodiments of powerful grace and freedom in the face of a world bound by the Law. I remember my mentor, Dr. Rod Rosenbladt, once saying that a masculine man "is a foggy or an out-of-focus picture of what God is like." Essentially, a masculine man is grace and freedom to those he encounters. The parable of the prodigal son is a good example. When a young man hears the story of the prodigal son, to which character does he relate? He doesn't want to be the petulant younger son. He doesn't want to be the whiney older son. He is drawn to the father. Why? Boys relate to the father because he is powerful, authoritative, credible and worthy of trust, gracious, kind, and forgiving. In short, the father is masculine. He uses his masculinity not to ridicule but to forgive, and in so doing shows himself to be that "foggy picture" of God to all who hear the story. We need more masculine men in our world to be that analogy of God to those who don't seem to see Him anywhere else.

## Pete

So too, in our lives, we sometimes encounter men like someone I once knew—we'll call him Pete. We all knew there was something different about Pete, something that made him stand out. To be honest, from his physical appearance, there wasn't much that was different about him, at least nothing that any man today would find reason to boast about. In fact, Pete was unassuming in his stature and looks. He was somewhat shorter than most men, was beginning to lose his hair, and had a peculiar habit of running his tongue along his upper teeth before he would speak. If you were to pass him by in a hurry, you would hardly give him a second thought. And yet, if you were to spend just a few moments with him, you would find that there was truly something different about him. Pete possessed a strange ability to transform a room simply by walking into it. His presence, his calm and purposeful movements, and his words always changed the dynamic of whatever space he occupied.

Something has been lost along our current path of moral enlightenment. We have lost something that leaves a giant void in the heart of modern culture. In fact, I would argue what has been lost is the truth that we need men to be men. We need men like Pete. We need men to be masculine. Further, every family needs a father who is masculine and who understands what it means to be a strong and gracious father. Clearly, we do not need men who are abusive, overbearing, stagnant examples of male domination and chauvinism. Undoubtedly, we could do without those who think that women are lesser by design and unworthy of our respect, dignity, or care. But it's equally clear that we have lost something when we allow the pendulum to swing so far to the other side, pushing men to be feminized, confused examples of insecurity.

In such a culture, it has become difficult for us to identify what exactly it means to be masculine. But we recognize it when we see it. Masculinity is something quiet. Those who are masculine are not mean or loud, and they will never be perceived as blowhards. They are typically unassuming in their demeanor. In turn, they are not moralists per se. Sure, they know the difference between right and wrong, and they will stand up for the right and fight the wrong. Yet their sense of right and wrong leads them to neither sanctimoniousness nor self-righteousness. Rather, their sense of right and wrong will, more often than not, lead to forgiveness. Masculine men are capable, strong, confident, and gracious.

---

### Radiators and Hair Buns

On Monday evening, my car (a 2000 Jeep Grand Cherokee) began to overheat. Pulling into a parking lot near my home to look for the problem, I found a small river of coolant pouring from the water pump and pooling beneath the vehicle. I risked driving it the rest of the way home but knew that my Tuesday would be significantly spent covered in grease and grime.

By Wednesday morning, my vehicle was on the road again after I replaced the entire cooling system, radiator, water pump, and thermostat and changed the transmission fluid and filter. After it was all done, a friend asked me if I liked doing that kind of work. I found the answer wasn't all that easy. I didn't like spending my day lying on my back covered in transmission fluid.

I didn't like making three trips to the auto parts store. I didn't like busting my knuckles when the torque wrench slipped off a housing bolt. But I loved the quiet victory of being able to master my own stuff.

It wasn't just that I fixed the problem. It was that I gave it a shot. I opened the garage door, pondered the Chilton's repair manual, took a deep breath, and began to turn the wrench on stubborn bolts. Even if I had failed to fix it and had to take it to an expert, I would have found some joy in knowing that I went down swinging. That is what I liked, and I have found that I like that more and more.

But this doesn't just apply to turning wrenches. For the past few months, I had to take my youngest daughter to her ballet class. Not only did I need to make sure she was dressed and ready to go, I had to put her hair up. And I'll be damned if I wasn't going to figure out how to master the ballet bun. Trust me, at times, it was easier to change out a water pump than to control all the flyaway hairs and get the bobby pins to stay. I even watched YouTube videos for tips and tricks; by the end, I was pretty good at it.

I fear we have become accustomed to deferring to others, not just with our stuff, but also with our various callings in life. Too often we don't even try to master our craft (whatever it may be); instead, we settle for mediocrity with a few gems we've stolen from Pinterest or our Twitter feed to spruce up our work. What happened to a pursuit of quality? What happened to the drive to be the best at what we do? What happened to the willingness to risk failure so that we might be better in the end?

It's time to take some risks. It's time to shake off the dull sloth of what this world gives us and dare to master the stuff in our control. If you're a mother, then be one that breaks the mold. If you're a teacher, then be one that truly inspires. If you're a preacher, then be the best damn preacher you can be. And if you fail, who cares? At least you went down swinging. Besides, your salvation does not hang in the balance; your eternity is not fashioned by your hands. Only the blood of the Lamb decided that. You are saved by grace alone: so you are free to work, free to fail, and free to get up again and again. So get out the toolbox, roll up your sleeves, and do the work our Lord has given you to do.

Rev. Paul Koch

These men may not know the answer to every question or how to fix every problem, but they see themselves as capable of figuring it out. Further, they see it as their vocation to try! Try to do what? Try to handle what they have been called to be: husband, lover, father, worker, citizen, and friend. They don't always handle things the way they should, but they try. And when they can't, they are confident enough to ask a brother for help. When these men fail, they seek forgiveness. When they succeed, they find a small sense of pride in having been, even for a brief moment, what God has already said they are. This is not a complicated picture; it is actually kind of simple. Perhaps it is the simplicity that makes men stumble. Our culture has made us afraid to ask about masculinity. We, in turn, create pictures of it that seem so complicated and so nuanced that we fear that it is too difficult a goal to achieve. Fear drives us to avoid masculinity and everything it may imply like the plague. The simplicity of just being what God has declared we are—free—seems too heavy a burden to bear because we might fail.

## Philia

Masculine men have a true sense of brotherly friendship and love, or philia. They will find other masculine men with whom they surround themselves: men they know they can trust. It sometimes seems that masculine men run in herds because they are often together. This is not some sort of gang mentality; rather, it is iron sharpening iron. In the ancient world, philia was considered to be the most praiseworthy of all forms of love. This "friendship" was to the ancients seen as the cornerstone of the development of virtue, while our modern world, by way of contrast, completely disregards it.[1] In our social media–encumbered world, there are few who find virtue in true friendship. Few find virtue in friendship because few have actually experienced real masculine friendship for themselves.

This is why movies like *Tombstone*, *Braveheart*, and *Band of Brothers* are so popular with men. Men watch these movies repeatedly just to get a glimpse of what it means to be surrounded by a gracious masculinity that gives, sacrifices, and saves. Men need mutual support to teach them to be men, especially in our day, and our children need to see it too.

But these characteristics are not what changes a room simply by entering it. They do not explain why Pete stands out from others. So then what is it? The room changes when a masculine man enters because of the sense of grace that he brings with him. His unassuming, strong, confident, capable, and forgiving character seems to pour forth from his pores like sweat on a hot day. He is strong, but his strength is not used to abuse; it is used to protect and save. He is confident, yet his confidence is not used to demoralize. A masculine man's confidence is shared so that your confidence in him becomes a reassuring portion of your confidence. He is capable, but his capability is not used to demonstrate other's uselessness. He is not a moralist; rather, he forgives, confidently, capably, and seemingly unassumingly. A masculine man can forgive as much with a gesture as with his words.

## What about Pete?

Pete wasn't a big, loud, or impressive man, but he was different. He was a leader among men, and he led with forgiveness. In his career, he was respected, valued, and easily promoted. Yet he was the type of man who would volunteer to teach a Sunday school class because he believed that children needed more than moralizing Bible stories told by well-meaning church ladies. He knew that if men like him didn't step up, the Church would be left with scarcely more than rooms full of little well-behaved Pharisees. Children need to learn and see grace on Sunday morning in real ways, and Pete knew it. He believed and simply acted on his conviction that being a man means something of importance when the gifts of God's grace and forgiveness are being taught to children. Pete wanted to be sure that somebody was there to "hand over the goods" of the Gospel. Pete was just the man to do it.

So what is the problem? Why does it seem that men like this are in short supply? The real struggle is that to be a masculine man in a modern family is difficult. Our culture has been traveling down the path of feminization for more than forty years. Everything seems to have been feminized: fashion, art, music, the workplace, the home, the family, and the men that call themselves husbands and fathers in those families, too. It is not the fault of the women who desired to attain equal rights, which they should have had all along. It is the fault of the men for trading in their grace and power as the sacrifice meant to "buy back," as it were, a sense of equality. The result is that men have become passive in the culture, the workplace, and, tragically, the home.

Robert Bly, in his book *Iron John*, was the prophetic voice of this coming reality some twenty years ago. Therein he writes, "Some women want a passive man if they want a man at all; the church wants a tamed man—they are called priests; the university wants a domesticated man—they are called tenure-track people; the corporation wants a team-worker, and so on."[2] Fast-forward nearly a quarter of a century and what we discover is a world where the hyperbole of Bly's prediction is true. Males portrayed in our popular media today are of two types: the first, impotent (ten Viagra commercials a night seems overboard), dismissible, and stupid, and the second, homosexual and worthy of admiration. We have come so far and allowed the pendulum to swing in the complete wrong direction. Impotent and homosexual does not equal a man or masculinity, and it certainly doesn't lead to fatherhood.

A masculine man is not what our society seems to want. Rather, it clamors for a passive man, and that is exactly what it gets. Our world is full of men who are either passive, angry, or both. What is worse than an angry, passive-aggressive man? Furthermore, passive men do not make good fathers; in fact, they may not want to be fathers at all. Again, Bly has insight: "The passive man may skip over parenting. Parenting means feeling, but it also means doing all sorts of boring tasks, taking children to school, buying them jackets, attending band concerts, dealing with curfews, setting rules of behavior, deciding on responses when rules are broken, checking on who a child's friends are, listening to the child's talk in an active way, et cetera."[3] Being a dad is hard. As a dad, you may someday be called on to change a diaper, go to a parent-teacher meeting, or, God forbid, sit next to a hospital bed with a desperately ill child. It doesn't seem sexy or exciting to be a dad; certainly, it doesn't seem to be masculine. Dads who have little girls may even be called upon to do their hair and attend tea parties with stuffed animals.

Furthermore, being a husband and father seems like it's a lot of work. Will the man who decides to go this route have time to work out and keep his "masculine physique"? Or will he spend his Saturdays fixing broken sinks, unclogging toilets, and running children to swimming lessons? What is masculine about that? Doesn't it seem more masculine to spend the day perfecting a rock-hard body, surfing, hanging out with friends, or planning your next coital conquest? Is the daily grind of handling family business really masculine? Is setting aside immediate wants in favor of helping someone else—your family—what it means to be a man? Questions like these are not easy to answer. To be honest, there is nothing about working out, surfing, or hanging with the guys that is unmasculine. But the heart of masculinity comes in relationship to others whom God has called us to serve.

So we are told by our culture that these burdens are to be avoided until the very last minute. Young adults are told to delay true, meaningful relationships in favor of casual hookups. They are advised to avoid marriage—especially young marriage—as long as possible. They are told to avoid being a dad until forced into it. But is this what men really want? Is this passive and fearful approach to life what women want of men? Our culture creates little to no positive mystique surrounding masculinity or fatherhood. For little girls playing with dolls and pushing strollers, Mom is a superhero. Little boys have no one to look to but cartoon characters and sitcom dolts on the television screen. As a result, most young men view fatherhood as something to be avoided at all costs.

## Who Is Minding the Kids?

A recent U.S. Census Bureau report titled "Who's Minding the Kids?"[4] notes that when both parents are home with the children, the mother is labeled the "designated parent." The report also notes that when Dad takes care of the kids while Mom is away, that's deemed a "child care arrangement." When Mom takes care of the kids while Dad is away, it's not a "child care arrangement"—that's just Mom being Mom. Our culture designates moms as parents and dads as childcare helpers. No boy I ever knew growing up wanted to be a childcare helper.

As a result, men don't talk about becoming fathers. When a woman tells one of her friends that she would like to be a "good mom" someday, there is more often than not a positive affirmation of her dream. If I tell my daughter that I think she'll be a good mom, she blushes and gleams as much as when I tell her that she's pretty or that I love her. If a young man tells another young man that he will be a good dad, there is a notable sense of discomfort that comes over the young man, a fidgeting nervousness followed by the exclamation, "Wait a minute, slow down. I'm not ready to think about that!" We have been conditioned to resist, hesitate, and shift the discussion as soon as it arises.

These unfortunate realities have led to a state of prolonged adolescence in young men. Boys refuse to grow up and accept their roles as adults and the consequent responsibilities implied. Again, the general message is that young adults ought to postpone marriage as long as possible—just "shack up" with each other. Who needs to get married? Kids are a hassle and restrain "my" options. Young adults are told that it is their job to have as much fun as they can while they are still young, single, and free, as if to say, "Once you've had all the fun you think you can have and you've put off marriage as long as possible, then you should get married and die." But as the parable of the prodigal son reminds us, such a life never quite turns out how we imagined. The Church, sadly, has been no different for the past few decades in this area. The Church and the people in it try to convince every young adult that they ought to wait as long as possible.

## Where Have They Gone?

Furthermore, where are the masculine mentors who are also dads? Those strong fathers, who have done that which we need most desperately, don't seem to be saying anything about how great it was.

Add it all together and this is what you get: young men don't grow up wanting to be fathers. They haven't seen strong masculine men as fathers that they want to emulate. If young men didn't grow up respecting men, it follows that they also didn't grow up wanting to be fathers. So why would any young man want to be a strong masculine dad? They can't aspire to something they know nothing about, something that they have never seen. Young men imagine being a dad as just another grown-up duty like changing the oil or unclogging an overflowing toilet; there is no magic, no wonder, no greatness portrayed in being a father.

Yet the father is by design the point of powerful grace in the house; his absence means that the apologetic picture in the modern house is bleak. Children are created to look to the dad in the house as a picture of God. God is powerful. God is authoritative. God is credible and worthy of trust. God is gracious. God is kind. God forgives. These, too, are qualities that we apply to a masculine man. The picture is complete. If the father is dismissed as passive and impotent and he is not to be admired, then maybe God is nothing to write home about either. But the reverse is also true: if dad is a foggy picture of God and is a good, strong, and gracious, then maybe God is good, strong, gracious, and maybe He cares about me, too. Strong men create strong and gracious fathers who, in turn, serve as an apologetic for a strong and gracious God who loves and saves freely.

No matter how much we try to set a list of characteristics to the word *masculinity*, we will probably never succeed in accurately describing the true man. The truly masculine man is more of a picture or an image than a list of characteristics. The idea of a masculine man is only fully realized when seen in an actual flesh-and-blood man. This is what Pete carried with him when he entered a room. He couldn't have provided a better description of masculinity than his presence expressed. In fact, he probably never thought about defining his characteristics; he simply lived them out while he strengthened everyone else. In fact, through his kindness, strength, and purposefulness, he helped those men around him to act on the masculinity they already possessed. Even if our culture, home life, sitcoms, and mentors have failed to help us know and treasure our masculinity, someone like Pete gave us the courage to simply live it.

Pete and others like him are living stories of what masculinity looks like. Stories captivate our imaginations; they take a hold of us in a way that a mere definition cannot. Stories inspire us to attain their standard. When we hear the story of a strong warrior, we want to be that strong warrior. When we hear the story of a good lover, we want to be that lover. When we hear the story of a strong man standing up against the system, we want to be that man. When we hear the story of a kind, compassionate, and gracious father, we want to be that father. Stories draw us in and motivate us to be more than we are. Every young boy wants to be the prince in *Sleeping Beauty*. Every teenage boy wants to be like Steve McQueen winning the race in *Le Mans*. Every man wants to be William Wallace in *Braveheart*, standing up for his own freedom. And every dad who hears the story of the prodigal son wants to be that father.

## The Father of the Prodigal: A Real Man's Man

So recall the tale of the prodigal son. A powerful man of means, who is also a good father, allows his younger son to seek a sense of desperate freedom. The son's freedom turns out to be a disaster, not because it is freedom, but because its root is desperation. The story begins with a demand. The son appeals to the law of inheritance to fulfill his demands. Yet in his desperation, he refuses to wait for what the law demands: his father's death. In this case, as in most, the appeal to the law is what produces desperation and fear. Desperation is fear, fear is of the Law, and this will always and only bring condemnation. The condemnation of the younger son leads back to where it began: more desperation. Now in his despair, the young son returns to the good father. The good father then takes his desperate son back. He embraces him, redeems him with his word, places him back into the family, and celebrates. Desperation is set aside in the father's forgiveness and replaced with true freedom. Freedom is a gift given in love, which is good and strong because it is free. It always requires more strength to make someone free than it does to keep that person in bondage. Freedom is of the Gospel and is given by the powerful Word of the Father. An older son appears in this story. This son whines and moans at the disparity, which the father displays. He sees the father's love as disparity because he too is weak. He is weak because his self-righteousness is also of the Law, and the Law always condemns. The father, again, steps in and redeems the older son with his strong grace and his powerful Word. His powerful Word is freedom, it is the Gospel, and it is strong and masculine.

Which is the more masculine character in the story of the Prodigal Son? Which of these three men changes a room merely by entering it? Is it the petulant, demanding, and debauched younger son? Is it the whiney, self-righteous, and self-important older son? Or is it the waiting father? Paint the image of these three men in your mind. Which paints the picture of a real man? Petulant, whiney, weak, debauched, and desperate—is this the description of a masculine man? Strong, kind, merciful, declarative, compassionate, gracious, and inspiring of true awe and respect—this is the true portrayal of a masculine man. The father in this tale is the man; the other two are yet boys. Boys can be weak in their immaturity. In fact, we expect boys to be weak because they are only still learning to be strong. Over time they may become strong and masculine, but not while they are self-absorbed, impatient, and needy. Until they overcome this self-absorption, they probably aren't ready for marriage or fatherhood.

The father in our story is what true masculinity is meant to be. He is not brash. He is not overbearing. He is not demanding. Nor is he a disciplinarian of a higher order than mom. Rather, he is kind, strong, compassionate, gracious, and thus inspiring of awe and respect. His words have power because they are of the Gospel and not of the Law. His words produce freedom, allowing those he influences to be free and to be masculine in return. He is not only a picture of the Father; he is a picture of what it means to be a masculine man free of chauvinism but full of masculinity, full of grace. People that we know or have known who are like this are illustrations of quiet, strong, gracious, and forgiving masculinity. In our imperfect and broken lives, we cling to and are driven by images like these. The father in the parable gives us the courage to be the men God has called us to be: to love, be gracious, share the Gospel of forgiveness, and set others free. It is time for men to stop being desperate and to be free. Men need to know that they are free to be what God has created and called them to be: confident, gracious, forgiving, masculine men who are analogies of God to those who don't seem to see Him anywhere else.

# CHAPTER 4

# When a Man Loves a Woman

*When a man loves a woman*
*Can't keep his mind on nothin' else*
*He'd trade the world*
*For a good thing he's found.*

—Percy Sledge

I'm not generally a Percy Sledge fan, but when I began writing this chapter, I was celebrating my twentieth wedding anniversary and listening to this song, written by Calvin Lewis and Andrew Wright, and I was feeling a tad sappy. Meeting my beautiful wife was like hitting a brick wall at sixty miles an hour. I simply didn't know what hit me. I think that falling in love is kind of like that—something you don't control and something that is unexpected. When I look at my wife, I believe that God created her to cause me to say, "Wow," when I see her. And twenty years later, the sight of her naked body still causes me to say that same "Wow"! He created her to long after me, desire me, and, further, to desire my desire of her. I believe that God created me to want to care for her, protect her, love her, and desire her more than anything. And desire her I do! As time passes, love settles in, and it's less of a surprise and more like something you can't remember being without. Over time, love grows, and its desire and need grows along with it. And then as two people, husband and wife, grow together, they begin to realize that they want more together.

The marriage relationship is a special one. It is more than sexual, though it is sexual. It is more than emotional, though it is highly emotional. It is more than a commitment, though it certainly is that. It is hard. It is wonderful. It challenges and it rewards. It makes one tired and it fills one with a never-ending energy. It embodies all the wonderful aspects of our world while at times challenging us with some of the most intensely negative aspects of our inner thoughts and feelings. It is a picture or snapshot of our life and faith. It is a wonderful mystery. When a man loves a woman, he really can't keep his mind on anything else. She becomes so much a part of who and what he is that it is difficult for him to tell where he ends and she begins. Paul says much the same in Ephesians: "In this same way, husbands ought to love their wives as their own bodies. He who loves his wife loves himself."[1] As God describes the love of a man for his wife as He describes marriage, He tells us that the two literally become one flesh. They are the primary family relationship because they are one. He is transfixed on her, and she is enthralled with him.

Think of Adam, awaking from his slumber and rising from his bed. He takes in the beauty and blessing of the day. He stands upright, proud and strong as the pinnacle of all creation. Fashioned in the image of God, he is given lordship over all that his eyes behold. But this morning, this awakening, is unlike any other. He beholds a creature upon which he had never before laid his eyes. Perhaps in dreams alone he imagined such a creature, but there it is standing before him. Rather, there *she* is. He rushes to her, embraces her, and sings out the first song of creation. He says, "This at last is bone of my bones and flesh of my flesh; she shall be called Woman, because she was taken out of Man."[2]

Yet when the two become one flesh, they are also called to become more than two whenever possible. They are called to make babies. The consequences of this are profound. I sometimes consider alternate scenarios. What if Joy and I had not met during that summer at Arrowhead Lutheran Camp in 1993? Well, we would have never been married. We would have never had our children, Caleb, Joshua, and Autumn. Caleb would have never met his wife, Erika. Their future children (God willing) would never be born, and so on. Our union, now twenty years ago, had consequences that we could never have dreamed of, eventually leading to an untold number of lives down the road in future generations, more marriages, more new babies being born as a result of our marriage, an ineffable number of baptisms, and new lives being washed in the blood of Christ.[3] The marital relationship is the primary relationship in a family. Marriage is the foundation upon which a family is built.

So then, these two, husband and wife, are called to be one flesh, but they are also called to be father and mother. These are dramatically different roles. Not only do parents bring children into the world; they are also called to bring them into the family of God and to the Faith. They not only sustain the physical lives of their children; they also bring them to the baptismal font and to the Word. They teach them and train them in life and in the Faith. As the Proverb says, "Train up a child in the way he should go; even when he is old he will not depart from it."[4] Parents teach their children both the Law and the Gospel. Even in who they are as mothers and fathers, they teach them about the Law and Gospel. Parents serve as denotative pictures of these concepts in the home. They bind and set free, wound and heal, give guidance and let go. They are the most powerful force in shaping the men and women their children will become. So if moms and dads do this together, why is there no mother in the parable of the prodigal son? So far, I have used this parable as the ultimate story of "God-centered" parentage. How are we to understand their significant and distinct roles when mom is absent from this parable? We are left to wonder. I think I might have some insight. Reconsider the parable of the prodigal son as told by a mom. Imagine that these events occur while dad is away. The parable might resemble something like this. I give you "A Mom and Her Two Boys."

## A Mom and Her Two Boys

I knew a woman who had two sons that were in their early twenties and still lived at home. She knew that it was just a matter of time before one of them would decide to grow up and move on to live a life outside of her home. That day finally came, and her youngest son, her little baby, announced he was moving out. However, it did not go as planned. He was so rude in his approach. He left a giant mess in his old room. Furthermore, he demanded she pull $35,000 out of her retirement account and give it to him so that he could get off on a good start.

When she heard this news, she was very sorrowful. She begged her younger son not to go. Nevertheless, she disregarded his rudeness, cleaned up his mess, and withdrew the money. As she handed it to him, she again begged him to stay, but he looked her in the face and said, "I'm a grown-ass man now, and I don't need my mom to take care of me anymore. Besides," he said, "you can barely take care of yourself." She gave him a teary-eyed hug, which he quickly shrugged off. As he was packing the car, she ran back into the house, raided her wallet of her last little bit of cash, and handed it to him. She pleaded with him one last time not to go, but he didn't even look back as he grabbed the cash from her hand, revved the engine, blasted the radio, and peeled out of the driveway. He didn't even give a little honk of the horn or a slight wave of the hand as he drove out of sight. Just like that, her baby was gone.

His departure left a great hole in her heart. Sure, her older son still needed her, but her younger son no longer did. To add insult to injury, it seemed as though he not only no longer needed her but didn't even want her in his life. This was something she couldn't accept. In fact, she was in complete denial. In this delusional state, she checked on him every day, either by his Facebook status or by texting him. Most days he wouldn't even bother to respond. When he did text her back, his responses amounted to little more than one-word answers to her questions. Though one-word answers are commonly considered to be very rude, these little morsels of communication with her wayward son made her heart dance with glee. Just knowing that she was occasionally on his mind made her happy enough to carry her through a few more days.

Sadly, even his random one-word text responses stopped. She heard not a word for several months—no Facebook updates, no Twitter tweets, no Pinterest pins. There was nothing she could find to give her hope that he was still alive. Yet one night out of the blue, she received a collect call at 2:00 a.m. "Mom," he said, "You need to wire me some money right now." He added, "I got pulled over for a DUI here in Atlantic City, and my car was impounded." She told him not to worry; she would take care of everything. He hung up the payphone at the police station without a word of thanks. Nonetheless, she did what he asked and wired the money to both bail him out of jail and get his car released from the impound yard.

She didn't hear from him again for almost a year. Nonetheless, she continued to keep her eye on his status and made sure to text him regularly, letting him know that she was remodeling his room for when he was ready come back home. About a year later, he called her again, this time telling her that he would be home in an hour and that he was bringing his new partner, Sebastian, with him. They would need a place to stay, as their landlord kicked them out for failure to pay the rent.

The mom looked at her elder son and told him to pack up his stuff and get out of his younger brother's newly remodeled room because he was coming home. The older son looked his mom straight in the eye and shouted at her, telling her that there was no way he was moving back into his old room. "It is too small and it doesn't even have the connecting bathroom," he exclaimed. "This is not fair!" After all, he is the one who stayed. He cut the grass for her. He fixed her car when it broke down last month. He is the one who helps around the house cooking and cleaning. To the older brother, this entire situation seemed like the greatest of indignities. How is it that his younger brother just gets to come home, no questions asked, and gets the bigger room with the bathroom?

She calmly, politely, and patiently told her eldest not to worry. She explained to him that she had already called the contractor to have a bathroom added to his room as well. Nonetheless, she needed him to move out now. Her final words sealed the deal: "Your brother is coming home. I will have my family all under one roof again. You should be happy that this makes me happy."

Is this how it might have gone? Maybe, but more likely the mother wouldn't have allowed her younger son to go at all. Instead, she would beg him, bribe him, entreat him, and plead with him to stay home so that she could continue to keep him in her care. Moms care for, protect, look out for, coddle, and remove obstacles from the path of their children. This is their calling and task. They teach them to eat, drink, and wipe their soiled bums. They bring order and rules to the lives of their young children. They keep the chaotic world of the everyday home to a low roar. They are the queens of their castle, and no one, not even the children themselves, will take their "babies" from them. Moms do all this, but they, for the most part, are not called to be the purveyors of freedom. There are always exceptions to every rule, but for the most part, a father is needed for this.

## Not the Same Order

Admittedly, fathers do not often bring the same sense of order to a home that mothers do. Sometimes they restore justice with their booming voices and extra strength. Sometimes they provide fun. But fathers are intended to provide grace and freedom. In order to be free, the son must first leave the home. He must be given what he demands and allowed to run his course with it. Also, the older son must be free to stay home and work for the family. Coddling them is no freedom. Providing the opportunity for them to be what they are is freedom. When children fail—and they will often fail—grace and forgiveness is then what's needed. Just as when we as fathers fail to grant them forgiveness, we too need to be forgiven for our sanctimony and lack of grace.

The son in "A Mother and Her Sons" was never actually set free. He was checked on, doted over, bailed out, and coddled. He never reached the point of utter despair of the Law that comes from being totally sinful and unclean and realizing it and repenting. The Law accuses those who are in their sin. We are bound by our sin and separated from God. We are totally depraved. We are separated from God and cannot, of our own accord, apart from Christ, approach Him. We are stuck where we are. We are they who look at a kind and gracious father, wish him dead, and demand he gives us what we are owed. And He does. If we demand to be put out of the family, He bows His head and allows us to leave. Yet He is, in the words of Helmut Thielicke, the waiting Father. He does not demand our return, but He does eagerly await our return.

The magic and grace in a father's love, which reflects that of God the Father, is that it desires love. Love necessitates that the thing desired most—love—can be lost. Moms often have a difficult time allowing the possibility of lost love and furthermore lost need. There is no mother in the parable of the prodigal son possibly because she would not allow the risk of her son's love being lost. For that, a father is needed. A father is needed both to allow the possibility of loss and, in turn, to give the gift of grace and forgiveness. To be adopted back into the family, one must first be allowed to leave that family. Or to put it in more biblical words, in order to be raised from the dead, one must actually first be dead. This is the thrust of Ephesians 2:5: "Even when we were dead in our trespasses, [God] made us alive together with Christ—by grace you have been saved." Many passages bear this hard reality. Yet we know that our waiting Father scans the road for our return.

### A Mother's Love

This past year has been a rough one for me. I love my children. I love babies. I adore a young 'un who looks up to me, pulls on the leg of my jeans, and needs me to help them with something. They might need something as simple as to be picked up. Oh, and can I pick them up! I fling them in the air so a rush of air pushes their hair back from their smooth little forehead and a smile erupts from their mouth, and they squeal with the immediate grasp of my hands around their little frame. I love children. To a mother, this is the best feeling on earth; need. They need something from us, and as moms, we are happy to give it.

But this past year has been a new time for me as a mom. My children are nearly grown. Most moms try to hold back the tears as their oldest goes away to college for the first time. Only mine didn't go away to college. After he had finished high school, he went away to work at summer camp in New York for twelve weeks. He planned to attend college at Concordia University Irvine (CUI), where we live and work. I had met my husband at camp, and I had that "mountain top" experience of getting to teach kids about Jesus's love for them day in and day out for ten weeks. So off he went. I wanted to call him every day. I texted him as often as I could because I wanted to know that my baby was eating well and getting enough sleep. I also wanted to know that he missed me. Shortly after he got there, he met a girl. Turns out he met his soon-to-be wife. She is everything I could have wanted for him. They are in love. After one semester away from each other, she transferred out to CUI, and shortly after, they were engaged and making plans for a summer wedding. Soon, plans of leaving the nest to live ten hours away were in motion. I broke inside. I should have had another "mom" opportunity: helping my soon-to-be daughter-in-law be a wife. Instead, I was about to lose being able to be needed by another part of my family.

They were leaving. They might never come back. I cried for three straight hours that Mother's Day morning. Their absence in my life destroyed my world for three months. I received wise words from my adoring husband to stop worrying and to be free and to let them be free. I needed to give them freedom for my own health and my relationship with them. But that isn't what we moms do. Rather, we worry. We worry about that child burning their hand on the hot stove and that child being a good spouse. We just want to make it all better. We moms don't want freedom; we want need.

It took some time for me at first to actually wrap my head around these things and to flip that switch from thought to reality. My husband was right. He was the voice of grace that I needed as well. I've heard him speak to our children often with these tones of forgiveness and graciousness. These words most times are really hard for me to wrap my head around, but here he was giving back to me what I needed. The love of a husband to tell me that I could stop worrying is hard to listen to. It's out of his love for me that he says that I could be free from my worry. I wouldn't need to worry because I have fulfilled my vocation as a mom and will continue to do so. It just won't be on a minute-to-minute basis anymore. It may be that it only happens a couple of times a year, but I'll be here when they call.

Joyce L. C. Keith

So how does this tie into the idea of one man loving one woman and making a family together? The truth is that God, in His wisdom, created us to be His male and female. He is the one who says in Genesis, "It is not good that the man should be alone; I will make him a helper fit for him."[5] He also gave our forefathers the first command to all creation, "Be fruitful and multiply and fill all the earth."[6] In truth, despite all our current social clamoring, which claims that there is no need for a father and a mother, telling us that we can "go it alone," God deigns that both be part of the picture.

To be sure, in our sinful world, this desire on the part of God often goes unheeded. Sometimes this is out of utter contempt for God's will and His Word. Other times this is due to untenable situations in which, on account of our sin or the sin of others, we find ourselves. Intentional single parentage, divorce, and homosexual relationships all push back against God's desire for us. The death of a spouse or parenting partner is also the result of living in a world deeply affected by sin. My own story is one of a child who was brought up by a mother alone after the death of her husband at a very young age. Mothers who have lost their husbands have it even harder, as they are forced into a position of trying to play the role of mom/peacekeeper and dad/grace giver at the same time. My own mother did this very well. In fact, if anything, she erred on the side of grace whenever possible. Yet this is not necessarily the ideal situation. The Devil, the world, and our sinful flesh cloud God's original plan. As Paul says, these sinful realities "press down the truth in unrighteousness"[7] and push back against the way God intended parenting to be.

The text of Scripture is clear: the intent is for a man and a woman to bring forth children and to raise them as a family together. The wife plays very important and essential roles in the family, both as a wife and as a mother. The clear reality is that one of the roles she serves is not necessarily as a shadowy resemblance to an all-gracious God who desires freedom and to be freely loved. The analogy only works because it recognizes both the need for freedom and grace even if that love risks loss of the loved one. All love involves the possibility of rejection. Risk is not coercive and neither is love. If risk is coerced, it is no longer risk, it is conscripted service. If love is coerced, it ceases to be love and becomes merely a set of programmed responses. In this love story between God's people and God, He takes on all the risk. In the love story between a father and his children, the father is willing to risk the loss of his children in order to love them freely.

Again, the salvation we receive in Christ is risky business precisely because it is so entrenched in God's love for us and because it is so free. It does not depend on us freely choosing, but it does result in our terrible freedom. Terrible because once free, there is always the possibility that we still sin again, and we will. The parable of the prodigal son always leaves me on the edge of my seat precisely because I know that he might flee his father's love again. In fact, having received the father's grace, it appears he is free to do just that. The possibility of a recidivist prodigal son is another reason, I think, there is no mom in the story. The possibility of losing a son's love a second time would be too much to bear for a good mom. I think it is fair to say that a mom would rather love than be loved, and maybe therein lies the difference.[8] God our Father desires both and has passed that desire on to those whom we call father. This is the apologetic magic in a father's love. A father both desires to love his children and is willing to risk being freely loved by them in return.

A good dad does not operate under the assumptions of the Law. The Law abhors freedom because freedom may lead to sin, harm, abandonment, and condemnation. This is, I think, what moms fear the most. Moms typically want it done right. They want to protect from the harm that freedom brings. Moms, on the whole, operate under the assumptions of the Law because they have to. This is not a glorious calling, but it is a brave and necessary one. Moms are called on to keep the house in order and make sure the kids are fed, dressed, and ready for the day. They keep the peace and clean up the messes. They are needed in the home as much as I need oxygen with every breath in order to live. Without moms doing what they do, the home would not be a place of peace and respite from the world—it would be chaos. Dads, on the other hand, are called to be models of grace and proclaimers of the Gospel. To proclaim the Gospel again means to offer freedom. This freedom is terrifying to those who operate under the daily assumption of the Law's proclamations of right and wrong, good and bad, the correct way and the incorrect way. What more terrible thing could be presented to the Law than freedom from it? Yet this terrible thing is exactly what the Gospel of Christ is all about. "Christ is the end of the Law."[9] The prodigal son is enveloped back into his father's grace, forgiveness, and freedom, not because it was the right thing for the father to do, but rather because it was the wrong thing for him to do. When was the last time your mom told you to do the wrong thing?

Mother loves her children because they were born of her womb; she feeds her children, cares for them, and has even developed a preference to be altruistic toward them, sometimes to a fault.[10] We know we love her because we need her, care about her, and even need her to care for us. Yet this is not freedom, so to speak, and it is not the same as a father's love. A father's love does not need or even care for the other in the same way. A father's love waits, forgives, accepts, lets loose, and sets free. There is really no value in thinking of these two functions of love in terms of better or worse. In other words, dad's love is no better than mom's love, nor is mom's love better than dad's. Mom's love is perhaps more like God's benevolent providence, pouring down light and sustenance upon us in ways we cannot even comprehend. In fact, its constant presence is perhaps why it is often easily overlooked. It is always there even when its manifestation is the voice of the Law.

The love of the type shown by a father cannot and will never diminish mother's love but rather will add to it because a dad's love is not of the type that is diminishing. A father's love is again a waiting and quiet love. It seeks to not take away from but rather add to. By being Redeemer, Christ's love did not diminish the love shone on us by the Father as Creator and sustainer, nor did He diminish the love of the Holy Spirit as Comforter. In the same way, dad's love does not diminish mom's love. Dad's love simply points to a God who redeems the sinner, frees the captive, and welcomes the lost. It is only our brokenness that might lead us to try to play the loves against one another as if both weren't aimed at our good.

So then a dad is most often also a husband. Or at least that is the way God intended it to be. The task of husband is not to alienate his wife by means of his gracious world but rather to wrap her into it like a warm blanket. Moms have a very difficult job. They are called on to meet the everyday physical needs of their children. Dr. Paul D. Fairweather was the founder of the Fuller Theological Seminary School of Psychology and the author of *Symbolic Regression Psychology*. In that work, he notes, "To elaborate, in the beginning the mother supplies the physical nurturance while the father supplies the spiritual nurturance to the child. That is, the father supports the mother's authority over the child's inner world. He affirms the mother's command, 'Eat your carrots.' At adolescence this is reversed. The father teaches and supplies nurturance for the concrete, practical matters of the outer world while the mother provides a spiritual presence, which supports the child to believe the father. She affirms the father's faith: 'Yes, you can get that job.'"[11]

The mother's task is then to have faith in the father so that the children will have faith in his confidence in them. A good husband's task concerning his wife is to extend grace to her as well so that his forgiving words, as often as possible, become their forgiving words. They have very distinct roles, but they are in this together. Again, as we were reminded in Eden, "It is not good for a man to be alone, let us make a helper for him."[12] When a mother properly carries out her vocation of caring for and nurturing her children's daily needs, this frees up the father to properly be the gracious and loving father, protecting, leading, and guiding his family.

Again, go to any playground and watch the parents. Who is encouraging their children to swing a little higher, ride their bike just a little faster, and throw just a little harder? Who is encouraging children to swing not so high, slow down, and throw not so hard? Fathers free their children to take chances and push limits and mothers protect and are more cautious. And this difference can cause disagreement between mom and dad on what is best for the child.

But the difference is essential for children. Alone, either of these manifestations of love can be unhealthy. One can tend toward encouraging risk without consideration of consequences. The other tends to avoid risk, which can fail to build independence, confidence, and progress. God's plan was for parents, mother and father, to work in concert.

As important as I think it is for a man to be a man and for men to be good fathers, it is more important to remember that the relationship of a man to his wife is the first and primary relationship in his family. It is because the two have become one that the one becomes many. His passion for her results in his protection, leadership, and guidance and in turn her nurture and care of him and their children. It is she that makes him a father and he that makes her a mother. If their relationship is broken, if he does not desire her or she him, their children will lack a model of how God in Christ loves the Church. Again, from the Apostle Paul in Ephesians, "For we are members of his body. 'For this reason a man will leave his father and mother and be united to his wife, and the two will become one flesh.' This is a profound mystery—but I am talking about Christ and the church."[13]

So we rejoice in our wives, and we say thank you for their support and care. We give thanks to God that we have been allowed to love, honor, cherish, and protect them. In their faith and encouragement of us, we find the strength to fulfill our vocation as fathers. Though this duty would still be ours without them, they make it better and vice versa. Our wives provide what we need and cause us to continue to sing the ancient song, "This at last is bone of my bones and flesh of my flesh."[14]

# CHAPTER 5

# On Being a Dad

*No word makes me happier than the word "daddy" when it's directed to me.*

—Michael Josephson

## Introduction

As I stated in the introduction, as a young man, I was struck by the lessons I first learned while studying under Dr. Rod Rosenbladt. Over the years, as my children have grown, I have attempted to make sense of and implement some of the lessons I learned in those cursory ways so long ago. Rod's mentor on the subject of fatherhood was the aforementioned psychologist and founder of the Fuller Seminary School of Psychology, Dr. Paul Fairweather. Paul would often tell his men's group, "We imagine that the West will fall because of the lack of fossil fuels. It won't; it will fall because of a lack of fathers." In Dr. Fairweather's time, he saw that such a state of affairs might happen. We can now say that it is happening or has happened. Paul described the father's forgiveness as the "obscure voice of empathy."[1] Describing a dad is like describing anything obscure; it's often easier to point to someone and say, "There, over there, that's a dad." You can describe something all day and still not get a true picture of what it is. If you were to describe a dog, you might say that a dog has four legs. If you see a three-legged dog, you would still call it a dog, but you'd, in all likelihood, say that it's a broken dog. In the same way, when we describe dads by looking around for something to point to and say, "There, that's a dad," we find that we have a problem. The problem is that we have a bunch of one-legged dads hopping around and it's hard to find one complete example in our culture.

Thus to begin, we look again to the parable of the prodigal son. From the parable I think at least five ideas can be examined. Some of these ideas have been examined in more detail in previous chapters, but in this chapter, I will attempt to weave them into a more complete picture. First, a dad is the model of grace in the home. Second, a dad is not a mom. Third, life as a dad is about raising children who are in turn gracious and kind. Fourth, fathers are strong models of grace in the home and thereby also models of the type of masculinity discussed in chapter 2 that is quiet, firm, strong, and forgivingly gracious and kind. Lastly, dads need to be forgiven as often as they need to forgive.

First, a dad is the model of grace in the home. The fact that we believe that the Gospel is true and that we have a Father who sent His own Son so that we could be His children necessarily affects our view of fathers and the other way around as well. There is a misconception out there that if children grow up to be "bad," it is because there was not enough law in their lives. Maybe, we think, if their parents had just been harder on them, stricter disciplinarians, they would have turned out better. I think the real misunderstanding is that we are blind as to how much law is present in our everyday lives. The world gives us plenty of law—law in abundance! What everyone, especially families and children, really need is grace. Fathers need to remember that we will never be able to give enough grace to offset the amount of law that our children receive in their everyday lives. It is just not possible. You may not even be able to hit the fifty-fifty mark; you'll constantly be in a deficit. We need more grace and more Gospel desperately. This is why the father in the prodigal son is such a striking figure. He does the unexpected; he hands out grace when our inclination is that more law is needed.

### Not-So-Cheap Grace

When I was in the seventh grade, I failed my first confirmation test. At that time, I was not taking confirmation very seriously and decided I didn't need to study. I completely bombed. This may not seem like all that big of a deal, except that my dad was the pastor of the church and it didn't exactly look good to have his firstborn disrespecting the youth director by not taking the class seriously. When I got in the car after class, my mother was fuming. My teacher had informed her that I had failed. She said, "You are the pastor's son and you failed confirmation! Just wait till your father gets home!" It struck me at that moment that I had failed not only the test but also my dad. What would people think about a pastor whose son disrespected the church staff and wasn't serious about learning God's Word? It does not reflect well on a pastor when he cannot seem to manage his own household well.

When I got home, I went downstairs and awaited my dad's arrival with fear, uncertain over what he was going to say to me. You might say that the law was working hard on me. I knew I was done for. So I was quite anxious when he called me upstairs to have a talk. "I heard you failed your test." "Yes, sir." "Don't you think you should have studied harder?" "Yes, sir." "OK. Do you want to go watch the game?" "Ummmm . . . yes, sir!"

Now, you don't know my dad, but in my home, the invitation to watch the game was as good as an absolution! He never brought up my failure again. He never once mentioned anything about how a pastor's son should act in confirmation. He just invited me to watch the game. His first move was one of grace and not condemnation. In this, he removed fear from my relationship with him. From then on, I knew I didn't have to fear my dad when I got in trouble. He was on my side. I knew I could trust him to never treat me with anything less than grace.

Some of you would accuse my dad of cheap grace or think that he went too soft on me. You may think he just showed me that I could get away with anything without fear of consequences. However, you should know that his actions produced the exact opposite result. His gracious attitude has, even to this day, produced in me a great respect and admiration for him. Especially now, as I raise my own children, I am in awe of how he was able to handle my brother and me with such wisdom and grace. I only pray that I can do the same with my children. Also, for what it is worth, I never failed another confirmation test.

Pastor Bob Hiller, MDiv

By using the picture of a father as the model of grace, the intent is not to imply that a mother is not a model of grace or that a mother cannot be gracious. Rather, the intent is to say that God calls fathers into the lives of their children so that through these fathers, the grace He shows to the world is modeled in a very personal and intimate way. Mom can be as gracious as dad, and dad does need to discipline, but not as often as you might think. It is simply that the defining aspect is not power. It's more like the New Testament: the Son obeys the Father because He knows that the Father's will is good. The emphasis here is one of calling or vocation, not of quality, influence, or importance.

Obviously, as someone who was primarily raised by women, I have through the years struggled with this concept. Often, as one who loves his wife with a passion unequaled this side of glory, I still struggle. But my struggle, or your struggle with these statements, does not make them less true. The father fosters and protects the sense within the family that everything is OK, because Christ has made it thus and he knows it. This reality is vocational and theological. Vocationally, the father's role in the home is to point children to the deliverance we have received on account of Christ through word and deed. Every move that a father makes with his children ought to be oriented around the understanding of this theological and vocational reality. Fathers, according to this view, are not called on to play the "wait till your father gets home" role represented by 1950s sitcoms. Rather, fathers are called to be as little Christs, as Luther would say, to his first neighbors, his family. Fathers teach grace and forgiveness to the family, wife and children, by what they do and what they say.

Second and correspondingly, a dad is not a mom! In other words, if you are a father, you are not a mother with bigger muscles and a deeper voice. Sure, mom will need your help on occasion, but the mistake is to believe that being the heavy in every family dispute is your full-time family-related calling. This sometimes unpleasant reality will occasionally put you at odds with your wife. The key is to remember that it is not you against her but rather that the mother has a calling in the family and the father has a calling in the family, and they are not the same. Again, this has often struck me oddly and caused me on occasion to be taken aback. Yet when I think about it, I often fall back on the words of Paul:

Even so the body is not made up of one part but of many. Now if the foot should say, "Because I am not a hand, I do not belong to the body," it would not for that reason stop being part of the body. And if the ear should say, "Because I am not an eye, I do not belong to the body," it would not for that reason stop being part of the body. If the whole body were an eye, where would the sense of hearing be? If the whole body were an ear, where would the sense of smell be? But in fact God has placed the parts in the body, every one of them, just as he wanted them to be. If they were all one part, where would the body be? As it is, there are many parts, but one body.[2]

Dad is not the bicep! The father is the head of the family and thus, as Christ is the head of the Church, is grace and graciousness to that family. That is what God has called him to be.

Third, there exists a great misconception in that we think we ought to raise compliant children. It seems easier to raise children who have always done what they are told when they are told. Yet when this is my desire, I try to realize that this desire is the Old Adam in me. This base desire is really the fulfillment of my sanctimonious pretentions of the Law. So I am proud to say that I think, on the whole, I have throttled that sinful desire enough to have raised gracious and kind children who know that they are forgiven on account of Christ. There is a well-known quote from Martin Luther that has always disturbed me. After a day spent away from the university and with his entire family, one of Luther's sons acted disobediently toward his father. The son's disobedience apparently persisted to the point that Luther became exasperated with his son. Luther then exclaimed, "I should rather have a dead son than a disobedient one."[3] I couldn't disagree more. Further, if we are to believe that the parable of the prodigal son is a reflection of God's love toward His children, neither do I think Christ would agree with this statement. Obedience is as necessary as it is obviously not natural; we are all sinners after all. It too is one of the greatest and most insuperable sources of suffering. A tremendous amount of thought, writing, and laying down of the law has been devoted to the question of its necessity and how far it should extend, and it has seldom been imposed with a gentle hand.

Being a dad is not summed up by requiring compliance or obedience; it is, at its most basic level, pointing your children to the God who has made it all OK and saves lost sinners on account of Christ. Your children are sinners, and they always will be. They will fail, and they will fail you. They will be disobedient, arrogant, and altogether awful on many occasions. There will be days when both you and your wife will want to throttle your children and punish them or ground them until Jesus returns. Nonetheless, you are a dad. As a dad you are that model of forgiveness and the analogy of God. Compliance and obedience are of the Law. The Law always condemns. Therefore, compliance equals condemnation. How can a father be about grace and forgiveness if he is rather about compliance, which equals condemnation? He can't.

It is necessary to clarify that this doesn't mean tacit approval of unacceptable behavior; it means forgiveness and graciousness. What is being argued for here is not antinomianism (lawlessness); it is for being a model in the home of what the Gospel is, and that is free forgiveness of sin. Children need some fences. But the fences we construct ought to be around a giant field, not a tiny yard. A dad's love is centered on grace but is not permissiveness. Rather, dads are to be graciously forgiving. Dads know the boundaries, which keep the world—and their children, for that matter—in order, and they enforce them. Dads ought to forgive when those boundaries are crossed. I have high expectations for my children with no predetermined assumptions of failure. Yet when I father well, those expectations are tempered with a goodly amount of forgiveness when the inevitable failure comes time and again. Being forgiving, however, does not mean being permissive, like a grandparent who says it will all be fine because he or she doesn't know the depth of a child's depravity. A dad knows his children's failures all too well, yet he gives grace. And at times, fathers need to be able to intervene and say, "You are on a dangerous course."

This is not unlike when your friend says, "Hey, brother, you're on a destructive path"; it's based in a philia love that is accepted. It's not that there are no boundaries; it's more about having a holistic view of the vocation of father. Be as gracious as you can without giving up the necessary boundaries. A good dad is one who really knows the child. It's not rule based, it's based on grace and freedom. A dad might get visibly angry with his child because that child has put himself in great danger. The deep desire of every sinful father is to crush it out of them, to terrify them so that they will never do it again. The Law always accuses. Our natural inclination is of the Law. We think that using or overusing the Law will make us feel better. Yet even if that is the case, it inevitably doesn't actually produce in our children what we think it does. The Lutheran theologian C. F. W. Walther warns that the preacher—in this case I would argue the father—needs to understand where his audience is. The Law is a siren song because we are as much of a mess as our children, and we feel the need to control them because we feel the need to control ourselves, but we can't really do either. Yet when the default is grace, the child will realize that the discipline, even the anger, is born from love and protection.[4]

The Lutheran Reformers faced the same arguments about the danger of telling the people of God that they were free before God on account of Christ. Many claimed that the Law needed to play a bigger role in Lutheran theology in order to "curb" the behavior of Christians. Lutherans resisted this role of the Law, and some resist it to this day. Fathers ought to resist it too. The Lutheran Reformer Philip Melanchthon responded in the *Augsburg Confession* by proclaiming that good works would naturally flow from forgiveness.[5] If we as dads want our children to be good, gracious, or kind, first preach, teach, and model to them the Gospel of Christ, which is God's grace and forgiveness. After all, we all know that compliance is not all that it seems cracked up to be.

Fourth, as discussed in chapter 2, fathers need to be masculine. Masculinity, in turn, does not need to be seen as a bad thing; rather, it is what a man was created to be . . . a man! This picture goes hand in hand with a dad not being a mom; that is, men aren't just bigger women. Sometimes men are coarse, gruff, rough around the edges, callous, offensive, brave, daring, careless, and quietly kind. A man will often say that he loves you as much with his gestures as with his words. A man will encourage you to be adventurous while mom is telling you to be careful, and that is OK. Masculinity is not about a man taking off his shirt and pounding his chest. Masculinity is about teaching the qualities of a man through being honorable, trustworthy, brave, and strong while being kind and forgiving all at the same time. Being masculine is difficult. But to be masculine is a laudable, not deplorable, goal. Our culture could use a few more— probably many more—masculine men to step up and be fathers.

Lastly, dads need forgiveness as much as they give it. Forgiveness for dads is necessary for their occasional—or even frequent—lapses of empathy and forgiveness. There is pressure to being a dad. Dads know that one word from him can deject his children. If mom is disappointed, children will often feel like that is the normal situation. There is a story of a son who came down the stairs one day and encountered his mom in the kitchen. The son was disheveled and on his way to visit a friend. The mother looked at the son and said, "Look at you. Your hair is a mess and your clothes are dirty. Go upstairs and change before you go out and get yourself in shape." The son promptly looked at Mom, gave her a kiss on the cheek, and walked out the door saying, "I'll be home around nine." A similar situation occurred the next day with the same result. The son understood his mother's disappointment but shrugged it off as Mom just being Mom. On the third day, when the son came down the stairs, the son encountered his father, who simply said, "You're going out like that?" The son was completely dejected. This is because fathers have more power through even obscure comments than they would realize. If they are dismissive, rude, or mean, it can have a deep effect on their children. But a dad who is mostly gracious can overcome the occasional lack of empathy and grace. Yet this dad too needs forgiveness when he is ungracious.

Believe it or not, the burden of being the model of grace in the home is heavy. I have lost my temper and been the authoritarian as much as I have been this idealized model of grace, and for that, I am sorry and ask forgiveness from my entire family. Too often I have demanded compliance when I ought to have shown mercy and compassion. Too often I have been the mother with a deeper voice and bigger biceps. Too often I have been suspicious when I should have trusted. Too often I have praised the use of the Law in my house over and against the need for the Gospel. I am a dad and a sinner. While I strive to be a model of grace to my children—and my wife, for that matter—I am far too often the very opposite.

Forgiveness too might be needed from the world that does not understand grace and graciousness. Forgiveness is scary business, and that freedom that comes from it is even scarier. When a father is forgiving, his forgiveness can often be seen as injustice. He needs to be forgiven for his perceived injustice. Remember back to the prodigal son:

Now his older son was in the field, and as he came and drew near to the house, he heard music and dancing. And he called one of the servants and asked what these things meant. And he said to him, "Your brother has come, and your father has killed the fattened calf, because he has received him back safe and sound." But he was angry and refused to go in. His father came out and entreated him, but he answered his father, "Look, these many years I have served you, and I never disobeyed your command, yet you never gave me a young goat, that I might celebrate with my friends. But when this son of yours came, who has devoured your property with prostitutes, you killed the fattened calf for him!"[6]

The older son is pissed off at his father because his father is too forgiving. Dads too are sinful. They ought to do their best to implement both Law and Gospel faithfully and with equity. But the Gospel is not equitable, and it sometimes meets people when they are in their own sanctimony and self-righteousness and knocks them straight on their ass. If a dad is the model of grace in the home, he, like the father in this story, will need forgiveness from those around him as he forgives. When we as dads face this opposition, our response needs to be the same as the father in the parable: "Son, you are always with me, and all that is mine is yours. It was fitting to celebrate and be glad, for this your brother was dead, and is alive; he was lost, and is found."[7] This is forgiveness upon forgiveness.

I need forgiveness, because I am a dad. I try, and I fail. My model is a model presented to me by our Lord, and He does what I often struggle to do: love endlessly. I have only one confidence: I am saved on account of Christ alone. Having found that forgiveness in Christ, I am now set free from the Law that binds me. I am free to be forgiveness to those God has placed in my care. I am free as a man to be a strong, gracious, and masculine man. I am free as a husband to love my wife and desire her love and affection in return. But I am a dad! Being a dad, I am thus free to be what God has called me to be to my children: a model of His grace in my home. I thank God every day for the gift He has bestowed upon me of being a pale reflection of His love to my children, and I ask His forgiveness for when I fail.

My prayer is that the forgiveness He daily and richly pours onto me is reflected through me to my children, not as I should, but as I am able, in that when my children look at me as their dad, they can imagine a God who is like their dad but so much more. This is an analogy of being. I know that the relationship between a good father and his children is not just like that of a loving God to His people. Yet I also know that it is not completely unlike that relationship either. I know that being a good dad can be an imperfect picture of the love, forgiveness, and acceptance that we receive from God on account of Christ. And this is why being a dad is so utterly important.

CHAPTER 6

# The Magic Kingdom

*Family life is the most "engaged" life in the world.*
*There is only one adventurer in the world,*
  *as they can be seen very clearly in the modern world,*
  *the father of a family.*
*Even the most desperate adventurers are nothing*
  *compared with him.*

—Charles Péguy, French poet

A word of warning—though this chapter begins with technical concepts, they are necessary in order to tie together many of the theological claims in this book. If you stick with me, I bring things back down to earth by the end of the chapter.

A little magic goes a long way. The kingdom of God is a magic kingdom—magic hidden in the life, death, and resurrection of Christ. The story of Christ is the story of the Gospel, or the Good News that sounds too good to be true. Discovering that this story is true is magic. Children need occasional encounters with this magic in order to pull away the curtain and glean a glimpse of what God has in store for them in Christ. The message that our God died to save us while we were yet at war with Him is a magical message. "But God shows his love for us in that while we were still sinners, Christ died for us."[1] This magic is revealed in the grace of the One True God through the person and work of His Son, our Savior, Jesus Christ. This is no less than the story that seems so excellent that it defies belief. Children need to occasionally see and hear stories that are similar to this—stories that seem too good to be true but really are true. They too need to have experiences that lead them to encounters with moments that seem like they are so good and so right that they must be wrong. To find out that something is happening that you believe is too good to be true is magic.

The magic that a good father brings into the lives of his children is not the same as what God has shown us in Christ; but it is a significantly powerful analogy to it. In theological terms, this is called an *analogia entis*, or an analogy of being, something that provides a comparison between two proportions. The great thinker and theologian Thomas Aquinas has provided some help as we attempt to work out how God reveals Himself to us.[2] The struggle is our inability to express or comprehend God's greatness and magnitude. Aquinas claimed that our human language, as we try to explain God, is neither univocal (using the same word in precisely the same way) nor equivocal (using the same word in different ways). Instead, as we, in our feeble way, try to discuss and understand what God is or what He is like, we use analogical language and denotative definitions. As an example, when I say that "God is good" and "my dad is good," I do not mean exactly the same thing. As the Scriptures tell it, God is good in a completely unique way; one that is, on the whole, beyond our understanding of the word "good." Yet when I say, "My dad is good," neither do I mean something that is exactly the opposite of what it is meant when I say, "God is good." These two statements are rather meant analogically. That is, I am using an analogy to get the point across or point to something or someone—in this case, a good father.

Our experience with good fathers is meant to point us to God the Father. God shows us a glimpse of Himself when He grants us the gift of a good earthly father. In this case it is the notion that the very being, or *entis*, of a good father offers an analogy by which we understand in a limited way, almost like a foggy picture of God. A child can point to a father that is good and say God is in some way like that.

At the core of a child's universe is the Father, and He will make magic happen. He makes sure that everything is OK and that the children are legitimate in his eyes, and his desire is their well-being. His is the magic kingdom, and He will come through on His promises. Earthly fathers are a picture or analogy of God to their children. Good earthly fathers will likewise come through on their promises in the end. And the little bits of magic and magical experiences that they provide reflect God's love.

This is not dissimilar to the idea of a Jungian archetype. The psychologist Carl Jung postulated an idea that there lies within all of us an idea of the ultimate good.[3] Jung's ideas have been extrapolated and expanded by several scholars. Most notably, J. W. Montgomery, in *Myth, Allegory, and Gospel*, relates Jung's ideas to the truth of the Christian claim.[4] Montgomery states that there are multitudes of disguised "Christ figures" in literary classics. Yet Montgomery warns that this is not to be overdone. There is an automatic tension between imperfect characters and the historic Christ. The truth is etched in the human heart beyond effacement. Yet we, as sinners, repress this. This is what Paul says: "For the wrath of God is revealed from heaven against all ungodliness and unrighteousness of men, who by their unrighteousness suppress the truth."[5] This knowledge nonetheless surfaces through symbolic patterns, and as folklore it "bubbles up." Yet sometimes literature can reflect the Christian story and trigger conscious acceptance of it. Carl Jung's analytical psycho-therapy identifies such redemptive "archetypes." These motifs can be found in the most widely diverse religions. Man looks to both the beginning and the end of history to the concept of "paradise."

Mythology and folktale are especially pregnant with archetypal significance. There is a similarity in the collection of myths from around the world: a flood theme and the slaying of monsters by an outside hero are nearly universal. If these are done well, they strike to the deep reaches of one's being and point toward Christ—who has fulfilled the myths and legends of the world. Even the American poet Robert Bly has noticed the power of the myth. In his book *Iron John*, Bly states, "Fairy stories are the major gift that we have received from the preliterate ancient world. They're wilder than Aristotle's ideas, deeper than Luther's complaints, more full of truth than Montaigne's prose, great as that is."[6]

The idea of a good father is too rife with archetypal significance pointing to the Father, who is now preparing a place for His children in His mansion. Who will come through in the end? Who will save everyone when all hope seems lost? Who will make right what seems so wrong? Who will deliver us to a better world? Father will. This is again what makes the story of the prodigal son so powerful; it holds deep archetypal significance for us. The father in Jesus's parable is the father we all long for deep inside, the one we know without knowing and the one we come out of the womb listening for so intently.

So how is this done? The first step is for fathers to realize that they are like God to their children. When a child gazes upon his or her father, he or she sees creator, provider, protector, and redeemer— not as a perfect picture but as the aforementioned foggy comparison. In his recordings, *When Good Fathers Die It Is Always Too Soon*, Rod Rosenbladt casts a spell over his audience as he tells them stories about the magic that his father brought into his life.[7] But he also notes that even normal fathering is magic to a child. As I mentioned previously, I never knew my father, so these magical moments in my case came from male family members, friends' fathers, and eventually mentors like Dad Rod. In the lives of my children, I cannot say that I remember being "magic," but I do remember just being their dad. I also remember a few magical traditions that I led them through along the way. I will share some of these stories momentarily.

There is a concept in literature and film called eucatastrophe. Eucatastrophe is a term invented by the philologist and popular storyteller J. R. R. Tolkien in his lesser-known essay *On Fairy Stories*.[8] He used this term to describe the unexpected turn of events that occurs at the end of a story. This twist often makes sure that the central character does not meet some dreadful, imminent, and likely disastrous fate. The word is formed by combining the Greek prefix *eu*, which means "good," to the English word *catastrophe*. The word, as used by Tolkien and others, points to the "sorting out" or conclusion of a drama's plot. Used apologetically, the term connotes a deeper understanding that goes beyond its literal meaning. It refers to the ultimate eucatastrophe that is the life, death, and resurrection of Christ, which turned the plot of the history of the world. It thus refers to our salvation. In literature and myth, a eucatastrophe is present when the author reveals to the audience that the final card played will be the ultimate turning point where redemption is finally won: The prince breaks into the midst of the kingdom now taken over by the evil witch. He defeats the witch and breaks the evil spell that has kept the princess and her kingdom in chains for over a century.

A good father provides this rescue. He is a eucatastrophe to his children when he breaks in and relieves the mother from a day spent at war in an attempt to keep the children from killing one another and destroying the home. Children relate to this because they need rescuing from the monotony of everyday life as much as the princess in *Sleeping Beauty* needed rescuing in the castle. The children are delivered, and so is the mom. The rescue that dad provides gives mom a well-deserved break. Such things are magic. In the eucatastrophe of a good father's even occasional deliverances, we see a brief vision that the answer to our real problem may be greater—it may be a far-off gleam or echo of *evangelium* (the Word) in the real world.

Approaching the Christian story as real, we should expect to see reflections of that story in the world around us. It should not surprise us that we notice these reflections in art, literature, music, and film. God redeemed us corrupt creatures in a way that we recognize through the familiar things of this world—that is, through a man, the incarnate Christ. Thus the Gospel message is at one and the same time a familiar yet alien story. It is a story that we recognize in our deepest regions yet feel is too good to be true. In this sense, it is so beautiful and artistic in its own nature that it is almost mythical, and that is a story of a larger kind. Nevertheless, this story is true.

Therefore, the message of the Gospel is the most complete of all possible eucatastrophes. Further, this story has entered into our history and occurred in real time and in real space. Its occurrences are locatable both chronologically and geographically. The birth of Christ really happened, yet it feels too good to be true. The crucifixion of Christ truly occurred, yet it feels too sad and desperate to be dealt with as fact. The resurrection of Christ is true as witnessed by the apostles and more than five hundred people at one time, yet we hold our breath on Easter morning desperately waiting to answer when pastor says, "Christ is risen," to which then we respond gloriously, "He is risen indeed, Alleluia!" The resurrection is that kairotic moment after our hopes, which were dashed in the despair of the cross, are raised with Christ in the hope of His own resurrection. The resurrection is truly the eucatastrophe of our story and His. It is a story that begins with joy, tests our trust in the middle, and ends in something too good to be true. As Tolkien said, "There is no tale ever told that men would rather find was true, and none which so many skeptical men have accepted as true on its own merits."[9]

Again, its nature as primary truth leads us to search for shadows of this deliverance in our world. God has called dads to be just that. God has called fathers to be deliverers of graciousness and to create situations that are too good to be true. If a dad provides some of these moments for his children, his children will have a much easier time accepting the truth and value of the story of their God and Savior, which seems too good to be true as well.

So then how do we create these little moments of magic? I love movies. Movies can be a sudden glimpse into what should be. I believe that there is magic in movies. Is this magic true? The answer is yes, if the author and filmmaker have spun the story well. I have through the years attempted to pour some of this magic onto my children. I have a picture in my mind of my eldest son Caleb, at four years old, waiting in line with me at midnight to get in to see *Star Wars Episode I: The Phantom Menace*. His face was aglow as all the older attendees looked at him as though he should be fast asleep in bed and at me as though I should be ashamed of myself for keeping him up so late. That night was magic! We stood in line, ate popcorn, and drank coke until we were nearly sick. We watched Obi-Wan Kenobi defeat the evil Darth Maul and talked the whole way home about how awesome it was. When I tucked him into bed that night, I knew that he would never forget that little dose of magic. Yet I didn't do it so that he would think I was magic. Rather, I took him because I love him and I wanted to share with him something that I enjoy. It is the freedom of the open sharing, the escape, the deliverance from the perceptions of the Law, and the time together in brotherly love that bonded us and directs him to seek more.

Throughout the years of raising our children, I have made this habit of attending the midnight preshow of movies, a tradition that brings a little bit of magic into our lives. This is part of the magic of being a father to my children, though it has occasionally led to some marital strife. Some of my most enjoyable memories are standing in line to see the Spider-Man movies with my younger son, Joshua, who from a very young age we called Spider-Man because he climbed everything all the time. He was very small and dressed from head to toe as Spider-Man waiting in line at midnight. Even through the mask, I could see his ear-to-ear grin, and so could everyone else. To this day, every time we go see a Marvel late-night movie, my daughter,

Autumn, dresses up as a character. I believe it is called LARPing (live action role-playing). As nerdy as this is, such moments are magic for her even as a teenage girl.

This shouldn't be as difficult as we often make it. Rather, it is just part of remembering what it was like to be a child. Children's lives are filled with as many day-to-day encumbrances as are our own—perhaps even more. Fathers need to remember how wonderful the occasional release from those encumbrances felt for them. In remembering, they may then find the desire to create secret escapes. Trust me as someone who was once a little boy when I say that staying out until 2:00 a.m. with dad while mom worries at home to see the most exciting movie ever is magic!

Another way a good father brings magic is by giving his children the unexpected and sometimes scary or dangerous yes. Roald Dahl has a funny little rhyme in *The Minpins*:

> Little Billy's mother was always telling him exactly what he was allowed to do and what he was not allowed to do. All the things he was allowed to do were boring. All the things he was not allowed to do were exciting. One of the things he NEVER NEVER was allowed to do, the most exciting of them all, was to go out through the garden gate all by himself and explore the world beyond. And above all, watch with glittering eyes the whole world around you because the greatest secrets are always hidden in the most unlikely places. Those who don't believe in magic will never find it.[10]

Mother worries about the safety of her children. She rightly says such things are not allowed. But father remembers the sense of freedom and adventure his own slightly dangerous moments once provided and says yes. The father can bring this magic by saying the unthinkable and the unexpected and by freeing the child to explore and trusting in them to come back safely.

When Caleb was very young, Joy and I took him to Legoland after it had just opened. One of my most vivid memories is of the racetrack where children could get a "driver's license" and drive, unaccompanied, around the course. Caleb wanted to do this with everything in him. It was a little concerning as the minimum age was five and Caleb had just celebrated his fifth birthday days earlier.

Also, as our children were always small for their age, he barely made the height requirement if he stood on his tippy toes. The best wisdom and cautious advice would have said he was too young and too small to do this—in fact, I had to argue for fifteen minutes with the attendant to make it happen. But the fact that I did argue, he did get a driver's license, and he did drive were the things that made that day magic. He still has that license hanging around somewhere; I saw it not too long ago.

### Road Trips

Some of my most treasured memories were forged on the open road, sitting shotgun with my father off on some adventure. These adventures ranged from epic skateboarding trips to the Vans Skatepark in Milpitas, California, to academic journeys to Concordia University to meet up with professors like Dr. Rod Rosenbladt. These road trips weren't family vacations but rather sweet escapes that I enjoyed personally with my father. These ventures in many ways helped shape and define me as a person.

The conversations my dad and I would have on the open road fueled the excitement of the destination ahead. In the car, I learned to question everything. Talk radio filled in as the white noise behind our conversations and often stirred up the new topic of the hour. During these conversations, I not only learned what my dad believed theologically, ethically, and politically but also was given a voice to cultivate my own understanding of the world. My father would not let my thoughts go unquestioned; I had to defend what I was saying, and if I could not by my own might come up with a defense, my father would lead me to the answers I was looking for. Keep in mind, I am not talking about an older teenage me; I can remember these trips with conversation in tow all the way back to as young as four years old. These conversations prepared me for the end of our journey.

Whether it was about how to pick the right line on my skateboard, how to mentally and physically conquer the next triathlon, or how to sit down and speak with scholars, my father prepared me by conversing with me like an adult. In this way, road trips with my father were freedom and little bits of magic. I was not bound by the limitations of being a child; I was given respect and a voice to be my own person and to question the world and learn from those questions.

My dad was not only my mentor training me in all walks of life; he was my best friend. I could confide my deepest thoughts in him and receive comfort. This is a relationship that maintains to this day as I am constantly trying to squeeze in time with my father between my classes and his work schedule. The relationship of both master and friend created a longing inside of me that wanted nothing more than to be an adult. The respect my father commanded not only from me but also from his peers as well as the joy he shared was magical. I wanted to become the expert of all things, the presence of authority and a source of joy to those around me. I can say happily that dream is becoming a reality through the guidance of my father beginning with the magical road trips and now as I study at Concordia.

Caleb E. Keith

To children, little escapes are great escapes. A couple of years ago we hit hard financial times. I was working on my PhD dissertation at home while my wife was working for a local business in northern Nevada. Our three kids were all homeschooled at the time. Homeschooling is great if you can pull it off as a family because it provides freedom for adventures while everyone else is suffering under the monotony of the modern school system. This particular year, Joy and I decided to give the kids annual ski passes for Christmas (we lived in the Lake Tahoe area). Now, we were all but broke and could not afford passes to one of the larger, more prestigious resorts. But we did manage to scrape together enough money to buy passes to the local municipal resort where the kids had been skiing since they were all in kindergarten. So we made it a tradition. Every Monday, Wednesday, and Thursday, we would load up the ten-year-old Honda Accord and head the short distance up the mountain. The kids would ski on the little runs they knew well, and I would sit in the lodge and write about Philip Melanchthon. (I may have had a beer or two as well.) This presented a lot of work for me and, quite frankly, for my wife Joy as well. These times were little bits of magic for the kids. In the grand scheme of things, it is not a major turning point in one's life to miss out on a little homework in order to do a little skiing. But for children who day in and day out sit at home with Dad as taskmaster or Mom as schoolmarm, escaping to the mountains to ski can seem as meaningful as Samwise and Frodo escaping from Mount Doom. In the case of my children, their call for deliverance was my voice at 7:00 a.m. saying, "Get your crap in a pile. We're going skiing." Shouts of glee would erupt from the bedrooms as tired eyes were rubbed to encounter not a day of requirements but rather one of deliverance and goodness.

Such moments are magic to children. Through these moments, they know that the too good to be true can occasionally be true. Children learn to look for these moments and even expect them. This type of expectation on the part of children is not petulance or entitlement. Rather, it is hope. Hope is that thing within us that searches out redemption, freedom, and salvation. If one never encounters hope in day-to-day life, one will never expect to find it anywhere else. If there is never a real worldly deliverer, how can it be true that someone delivers from sin, death, and the power of the Devil? It perhaps can be true, but will we expect it, look for it, or believe in it, in Him, when we meet Him? Providing these magical moments is essential for a good dad. This type of eucatastrophe is really part and parcel with what it means to be a dad. The unraveling of the mundane requirements of our everyday existence in order to experience deliverance to the good is part of being a dad. Vacations, fishing trips, driving in the front seat of the car—all of these provide moments of magic and deliverance. I think we greatly underestimate the apologetic nature of the little things dads do every day.

The party hosted by the father in the prodigal son at the end of the tale is an example of this. The party is not expected. The party is really not needed. Certainly, it would have been enough for the father to take the son back. Why was it necessary to throw a party? It was necessary to mark the sudden turn of events with an event of the highest proportion. The party was magic. No expense was spared. No time was wasted. The young son needed to be delivered from the mess he was in, and there was no better way to make his deliverance known than to throw a party. Our salvation is often described in this way. It is said that we will be invited to an unexpected feast. "The LORD of hosts will prepare a lavish banquet for all peoples on this mountain; A banquet of aged wine, choice pieces with marrow, And refined, aged wine."[11] "'Let us rejoice and be glad and give the glory to Him, for the marriage of the Lamb has come and His bride has made herself ready.' It was given to her to clothe herself in fine linen, bright and clean; for the fine linen is the righteous acts of the saints. Then he said to me, 'Write, Blessed are those who are invited to the marriage supper of the

Lamb.' And he said to me, 'These are true words of God.'"[12] The son had done nothing but evil. It made no sense for the father to take him back and even less sense for him to throw a party to seemingly celebrate the son's misdeeds. But the party was the sign of deliverance that the son needed to know he was still a son and not a forgiven servant. Dad Rod has a story that always reminds me of this. He tells it this way:

> After I got my driver's license, I inherited my dad's old four-door Buick to use driving to school. It was a "straight-eight," which meant it had a very, very long hood. I had pledged a high school fraternity and been accepted into it. The new pledges were allowed to "skip" a meeting and leave clues around the city as to where they were hiding. I had five guys in my Buick with me, and we were all drunk. I carefully pulled out of a "blind corner," and by the time I saw the '57 Ford headed toward us, my long front end was already well into the lane. He hit us and just lost a headlight rim so far as I could tell, but my Buick kind of "fell into pieces" from the impact. I phoned my dad and told him that I had been in a car wreck. He asked whether all of us were all right and asked where we were. I replied, "Actually, just a few blocks from home, Dad. But we're all drunk." He replied, "Stay where you are. I'll have the car towed and come to pick you all up." Later, after delivering all the guys home, we came into our house. He [wisely] told my mother to leave us alone, and we went into a private area of the living room. He asked how I was, and I replied, "I'm shaking." He said, "That's shock. It will be fine." I was in tears, realizing that what I had done was "over the top" in anyone's book. He had his arm around my shoulders and said, "You know what I think you need? I think you need a new car. Go looking this week, see what you can find, and I'll take my lunch hour to come take a look, too." And that was the end of the whole episode!

In this story, Rod had done nothing but evil. He was drunk, he endangered the lives of everyone in the car, and he ruined his car for good. It made no sense for his father to forgive him and even less sense to respond graciously by buying him a brand new car. But the new car was the sign of deliverance. Rod needed to know he was still a son and not just a begrudgingly tolerated housemate. For Rod, the new car was equivalent to the ring for the prodigal son, signifying that he was truly and forever his father's son. As Rod has written all these years later in the epilogues for this book, "Grace is the regranting of full inheritance after a colossal screw-up! It is even greater than mercy." And as my friend Kurt Winrich has often said, "Mercy is *not getting* what you *deserve*—it cancels the million dollar debt. Grace is *getting* what you *don't deserve*—it fills the empty account with a million dollars." Rod will tell you it was his dad's grace that day that made him a theist!

I recently attended a Mockingbird[13] theological conference in New York. During one of the introductory sessions, the conference chaplain, Rev. James G. Munroe, told a heart-wrenching story about his dad. This is his story:

> One of my very best friends is my sister. But when I was in the fourth grade and she was in the second grade, I would say that sacrificial, self-giving love was not at the core of our relationship.
>
> One afternoon after school, she and I were having a fight on the second-floor landing of our house. I punched her in the stomach. She opened her mouth to cry. And in that moment, without thinking, I grabbed a spray can sitting on a table.
>
> Some of you who are of a certain age will remember when it was still legal to use DDT in your garden. For you younger ones, DDT was such a dangerous and poisonous insecticide that it finally was banned.
>
> As my sister got ready to cry, I stuck the can up to her face and sprayed DDT into her mouth. At that moment, my mother appeared in the room. She saw what had happened, grabbed my sister, ran downstairs and out into the street, flagged down the first car that came along, got in, and raced off to the hospital.
>
> I went into my room, sat down on my bed, and waited. I waited for the end, which was not far away. After a half hour, the front door opened. I heard steps on the stairs, steps that I knew belonged to my father. I knew that the apocalyptic second coming and final judgment was about to happen—and that I fully deserved it.
>
> My father walked into my bedroom and stood at the door. He saw the guilt and the despair and the sorrow and the shame on my face. Then he did something that has permanently affected my life. He simply opened up his arms. I burst into tears and ran toward him like a shot, and he folded his arms around me.
>
> I can feel those arms at this moment. And I know whose arms they really are. They are arms with nail-scarred hands.

Luther once claimed that the father (and the mother as well) is a priest in his own home.[14] A priest is the one that makes the sacrifices and brings the miracle or the magic, the unexpected yes and sudden turn of events and unanticipated redemption to the people. The father does play that role for his children. If you had a father, tell your kids a story about that man. If you are a father, remind your kids that you remember what it was like to be a child and experience the wonder of little acts of magic, the Christmas where you received the unexpected gift. The surprise vacation or the midnight preshowing of your favorite movie are magic to children. Give your children little glimpses of the turning points that will tell them that it is going to be OK in the end. In so doing, the little magic kingdom a good father establishes is a foretaste of the ultimate magic kingdom to come.

CHAPTER 7

# The Father's Home

*As every normal man desires a woman,*
*and children born of a woman,*
*every normal man desires a house to put them into.*
*He does not merely want a roof above him and a chair*
  *below him;*
*he wants an objective and physical kingdom;*
*a fire at which he can cook what food he likes;*
*a door he can open to what friends he chooses.*
*This is the normal appetite of men.*

—G. K. Chesterton,
*The Wildness of Domesticity*

## A Safe Place

Chesterton's idea of home is my idea of heaven. As I write this book, I find myself thinking about the state of the home. I am not referring to the ongoing maintenance tasks, which seem to be ever present when one owns a home. Neither do I refer to the endless list of chores with which every home, and every person in the home, must to some degree or another contend. Rather, I am contemplating the actual state of the home in our modern world. Why is home so sweet, as the old saying claims?

I think that in all my rumination, what I have realized is that the home is the primary place where one engages, interacts, and shares life with one's family. Thus a home is a kingdom to every man in that for every good man and every good husband and father, the home is a psychological, physical, ethical, intellectual, and certainly spiritual habitat where they are unrestricted and therein free. It is in this freedom that one finds that they can truly sacrifice and truly give of themselves for the sake of the other, which in this case is their family. The home is unique in that it is that place where one can give of him- or herself without the risk of diminishing him- or herself. In fact, in the home, to sacrifice is not to make weak, but it is in sacrifice that we are proving the old evangelical promise true. Our small and, to our eyes, often inconsequential earthly sacrifices given in the home point to that primary sacrifice that was won for us, not of coercion or derision, but from freedom for freedom.

Parroting the words of Chesterton, I think that the home is the only place where a man can truly be free. The home and the family, much like our life in Christ, not only is a paradox but also solves the paradox that it is. It is where to suffer is to have contentment. The home is that place where commanding is obeying. In the home, to be the head means to be a servant. The family defines the home. The family solves the paradox of what it means to be a man and woman. "Then the Lord God made a woman from the rib he had taken out of the man, and he brought her to the man. The man said: 'this is now bone of my bones and flesh of my flesh; she shall be called woman, for she was taken out of man.' That is why a man leaves his father and mother and is united to his wife, and they become one flesh. Adam and his wife were both naked, and they felt no shame."[1] The family and the home give us, male and female, a place to live out this calling to leave father and mother, be naked and unashamed, and become father and mother to our family of children. This should not occur from coercion but in love and vocational freedom.

A good home serves another apologetic purpose. A caring and warm home reminds us that our God does not lack warmth or care. God the Father is not a passive father. He is the one who has laid the foundation for all families and thus all homes. "For this reason I kneel before the Father, from whom every family in heaven and on earth derives its name."[2] God names a good home wherein a father and mother act freely to make and keep a family. He names them with His own name. He calls that family and that home to be a shadow of what He is: warm, caring, forgiving, and mostly free.

The modern attack on home and family is an attack on Christianity in that it is an attack on God's nature, His character, and His name. As we abide all the attacks in our culture on mother, father, house, home, and family, we watch that which God has set us "free to be" drifting away from us. These are the great gifts that He has given us, and we should walk in them. These are the rewards with which He blesses during the season of glad tidings. Good families and good homes serve as pale reflections of God in His goodness.

The outside world is not free; the Law rules it. If the world cannot experience God's goodness, how can we think it can experience God's good news in Christ? If Chesterton is right, and I think he is, the only free place that a man has is his home. This is where a man is free to provide direct experiences of God's goodness in many forms that pave the path to the Gospel. Again, fathers are an *analogia entis* (analogy of being) of God's goodness, paving the road to the path of the Gospel for their children in the home.

An *analogia entis* is therefore—when a good father is present— also *analogia relationis* (analogy of relationship). It is therefore quite a difference to understand the father-child relationship as not only an analogy of being but even more dynamically an analogy of relation. Our relationship with dad is an analogy to our relationship with God the Father. This is an incredible contribution not only to an understanding of the father-child relationship but also to our understanding of reality.

It is not possible to separate the physical presence of a father from the emotional and existential need for a father's presence or a relationship with that father; they are too intertwined. It is also not possible to separate the emotional need of a place called home where we are free to do just that. Home is that safe place where we first taste love. If you have tasted love, how much would you have to be paid in order to give it up? Would you give it up for anything in the world? The home then is not only the place of freedom; it is where we are permitted to love freely. Fathers are intuitively relevant then in a home. Home is where fathers become epistemically valid. A good father in a loving home causes the Faith to make sense in ways that offer clarity to their children. In this way, children can look forward to the mansion that Christ says He is preparing for them. They will look forward to being home with Christ because home is of freedom and love.

## The Modern Oppression of Women

Changes in the structure of home life have not been a single event or series of events but rather has been a process occurring over the span of a great many years. G. K. Chesterton wrote extensively on this topic. He notes, "The recent controversy about the professional position of married women was part of a much larger controversy, which is not limited to professional women or even women. It involves the distinction that controversialists on both sides commonly forget. As it is conducted, it turns largely on the query about whether family life is what is called a 'whole time job' or a 'half time job.'"[3]

Oppression comes in many forms. The worst form of oppression is that which is disguised as freedom. Like men, women should be free to pursue higher education and a career if they have the means, the intelligence, and the aptitude. Yet they too should be free to pursue motherhood and wifehood with impunity. In short, women should be free.

College enrollment rates in the United States are soaring. It seems that our society has gotten to the point where one must achieve at least a bachelor's degree to avoid being labeled an absolute failure and have any relevance in our economy and culture. This is apparently even truer for women than it is for men. The Pew Research Center analysis of U.S. Census Bureau data shows that females outpace males in college enrollment. In 1994, 63 percent of female high school graduates and 61 percent of male high school graduates were enrolled in college in the fall following graduation. By 2012, the share of young women enrolled in college immediately after high school had increased to 71 percent, but it remained unchanged for young men at 61 percent.[4]

These statistics indicate something I think many of us have felt for some time. That is, our society had systematically diminished the role of women in the home and elevated the role of women in the workplace. This is not to say that college is unimportant for a woman if she desires to be a wife and mother. It can be very important to that end, but how many women are encouraged to attend college in order to be better, more educated wives or mothers? I would venture few. The real issue is that the liberation movement does not seem to have been a movement that accomplished what its proponents told us they intended. They promised freedom! Freedom and equality seem to have been trampled underfoot. I do not actually believe, on the whole, that women feel free to get married young, start a family, have children, and stay home and raise those children. Rather, they are so highly encouraged to pursue higher education and a career that the "choice" to do anything else is presented as no real choice at all.

I have seen this time and again in my personal life. My wife left college when she was pregnant with our first child, Caleb. We now have three almost grown children, and from Caleb's birth forward, she has both worked and not worked, though for the last eight years, she has been a stay-at-home mom. When she tells people that she did not finish her BA, they look at her with awe and dismay, saying something like, "Well, now that the kids are bigger, don't you want to go back so you can get a real job?" My daughter too has faced this scorn. She is now fifteen, and when people ask her what she wants to major in while she is in college, she will sometimes say literature, but other times she'll say that she is not sure she wants to attend college. Better yet, she expresses that she wants to be a mom. I often wish I had my camera ready so that I could capture for posterity the look of horror on the faces of those interrogators of modern women's liberation virtue.

So is the modern woman really free? I don't think so. She will be free when she is free to choose with impunity—and without societal scorn—what she believes is the virtuous path. Again, every woman that has the means, intellect, and aptitude should be able to pursue higher education and career. Yet she too should be free to choose a husband, children, and home. For those women who believe that they are able to choose both, I would encourage them to wrestle with what Chesterton posed at the initiation of this section. Is family life what is called a "whole time job" or a "half time job"?

As women freely make these decisions, it is my hope and prayer that they are encouraged to consider all the facts. I will not here make the case for higher education and career, as I believe that others frequently do that better than I. As for the virtue of working in the home, I think that there is much to say that is often left unsaid. The home is the place that babies are first brought to and laid safely in their beds. The home is the place where love and care grows between husband and wife, parent and child. The home is sometimes the place where men and women die. The home is often that place where the entire drama of that thing we so cavalierly call life is acted out daily. It is not as large as an office complex on the outside, but it is much larger in its qualitative reach and scope to those whom we love. And while I would not be the fool that insinuates that it is the only place where a woman should work, I would say that the home is the most likely place that contains the whole amalgamation of the human quality experience. As such, women should be as free to choose to manage a home as they should to be the CEO of a company. It is time that we admit that it is the home that contains the integration and absoluteness of our humanity that is simply not fashioned by any other incoherent experience within the outside workforce. As C. S. Lewis said, "The homemaker has the ultimate career. All other careers exist for one purpose only—and that is to support the ultimate career."[5] Being a wife and mother is honorable and ought to be listed among those free choices that the liberation movement sought to make available to all women. Once women are free to choose wife and mother again, men will be free to choose to be good husbands and fathers, as well as heads of their home.

## The Head of the Home

So who is the head of the home? American hierarchical sensibilities have been commandeered by what I will call the Teamwork Movement. The Teamwork Movement is exceptionally egalitarian in its approach to everything, including home life. Thus to even postulate the subject heading "The Head of the Home" must seem to some to be both a dictatorial and oddly transcendent proposition. This proposition may appear dictatorial in nature, because to have a head, a boss, or a leader that is set apart is an offensive anachronism to the modern reader. In turn it appears transcendent because in our heart, I believe we all know that every family needs a head as much as every body needs a head. The family is the oldest institution. Our idea of family precedes everything, including our modern notions of teamwork and egalitarianism.

So who is the head of your house? Some might say the man is the head. Others might say it is the woman or the wife in the home. And still others would, as I have mentioned, insist that there is no head, that life in the home is a "headless" team effort. In my research on fatherhood, one thing has become increasingly clear to me. When we as a society lose the idea of the man as the head of the house, we also lose the idea of what it means to be a good husband and father. Why is this the case? Because once a man's freedom and authority in his own home is taken away, his desire to serve that home in love departs at the same time. It is the freedom provided in the home that allows men to serve lovingly as provider, protector, sustainer, lover, friend, and forgiver. Once his "headship" is removed, by either usurpation or dispersal, his lack of freedom will inevitably lead to a lack of desire.

I once had a friend that would pick me up every Friday morning at 6:00 a.m. and take me to the men's weekly Bible study sponsored by our little church in Carson City. We would always talk about "church stuff" while we drove to the restaurant. One morning, we were discussing why our church body does not ordain women, and we were entertaining the idea that they might want to consider it a viable option. At this point my friend broke in and proclaimed that he did not believe that men should give up their "men-only" perspective roles as pastors and elders in the Church. When I asked why, his answer cut me to the quick. He said bluntly, "Men are inspired by freedom yet are lazy at heart. If you tell a man he is free to stop being a pastor or elder, he will stop and happily let the women take over. Yet if you tell him he alone is free to serve in these capacities, he will do it with all his heart." I believe the same is true in the home.

Chesterton claims that the definitive aspect of being the "head" of something is that the head is the thing that talks. Speaking, or being the one that talks, is risky business. Words have power. Words change things. Words move people in ways that we cannot even understand. Thus if headship is the power of speech, I actually think that we ought to bring back the idea of the man as the head of the house. In the home, the father needs this authority for one primary reason: he needs the authority to speak the words of forgiveness. Just as pastors need the authority given from Christ to forgive, so too fathers need to feel this authoritative freedom in the home.

In my mind, this does not lessen the role of the women or wives in the home. On the contrary, it only strengthens it. Again, relying on Chesterton, "The man is the head of the house while the woman is the heart of the house."[6] In this way, I believe that the structure of a healthy family is such that mother's authority is differentiated from the father's, not so much by its appearance, but rather by how the mother relates and complements the father's authority. The structure of the mother's authority is defined by how she relates to the father's authority—she affirms her own authority in affirming his. In other words, she is the heart of the forgiveness in the home while he is its mouthpiece. This seemingly dichotomous idea provides an energetic intensity of value to our ideas of headship.

At the risk of parroting my friend, I think I would say that men are inspired by freedom yet lazy at heart. If you tell a man he is free to stop being the head of the house and thereby a good, free, and authoritative husband and father, he will stop and happily let the women take over all these roles. Yet if you tell him he alone is free to serve in these capacities, he will do it with all his heart freely. Men want the authority that allows them to freely love and freely forgive and not lord that authority over their family. Rather, we want to be the talking head of forgiveness that is the mouthpiece of your heart. But we are lazy at heart; if you take it from us, we will happily sit on the couch and watch television instead.

## The Head of the Family Should Teach Them

So what would it look like if, as men, we were to act as the head of our homes? "You are to honor your father and mother. *What does this mean?* Answer: We should fear and love God so that we neither despise nor anger our parents or other authorities, but instead honor, serve, obey, love, and respect them."[7] For Luther, this commandment was the bedrock of all earthly relationships. Following Luther's ordering, Lutherans count this as the fourth commandment, and the first in the *Second Table of the Law*, which are those commands meant to teach us about our relationships with one another. It is faith in the God of the first commandment that works itself out in the love that father and mother show to their children in the home. For Christians, there is only one "law": it is the "great commandment"—love God and serve your neighbor. Paul states this too as he writes to the believers of the church in Rome: "'You shall love your neighbor as yourself.' Love does no wrong to a neighbor; therefore love is the fulfilling of the law."[8]

The Christian faith is such a free thing that it is not bound to any particular set of prescriptive rules. Rather, the Christian faith is active in love throughout all a Christian does in his or her everyday life. This is nowhere more the case than in the Christian home. When we enter into the married life and eventually the family life, our home is where we work out our daily vocations in love. Nonetheless, both parents and children often fall short of these calls.

This commandment is the greatest of the commandments in the Second Table because it encourages children to honor the teachings of their parents. If the father is the head of his house, then it is the father who proclaims the Word of God to his children in the home. He (and the mother) serves as the lips of faith to their children so that generations to come might know the faith and in turn pass it on to future generations.

It is in this way that we understand that there is no good work more pleasing to God than the faithfulness of a Christian home. It is faith and love that make the difference between an earthly house and a Christian home. Where the Word of God is proclaimed and forgiveness administered, God is present.

When the Christian faith is working in the love of good parents within the Christian home, there are no limits to the good works and services possible in their physical and spiritual nurture of the children. Ideally, for the daily needs and physical care of her beloved children, God calls mothers to administer the home. For the spiritual nurturing of the family and the home, God has called fathers to be ministers and priests to their own little chapel. And while this reality does not always work itself out in our modern society, it is the way that God intended. As noted in chapter 3, many things get in the way of this natural order in our fallen world. Yet the ideal is for these to work together as God intended. The mother supplies the physical nurturance to the child, whereas the father supplies the spiritual nurturance; that is, the father supports the mother's authority over the child's inner world.[9]

On a smaller scale, the home has all the problems and all the opportunities of the larger world. As the world is, it too is sinful. As the world is complex, the home too is complex. The home after all is no more than a group of close-knit sinners gathered together in one place. It is a society on the small scale: sleeping quarters, mess hall, church, toilet, courtroom, schoolroom, hospital, and playground all wrapped into one messy little package. In this way, the home is truly the right place for both Christian charity and Christian vocation to begin.[10]

The sacredness of the common life and the tasks to which God has called us in that life are clearly reaffirmed in the home. It is in the meeting of the plain, ordinary, and everyday needs of the family under one roof that we are called to be "God's coworkers": "For we are God's fellow workers. You are God's field, God's building."[11] It is the Devil, the world, and our sinful flesh that rob us of these simple pleasures. They would have us believe that we need to be about more glorious things. But it is in the nurturing of children and caring for a home that we truly see God's hand at work.

Luther often said, "For God commanded women to keep children well-disciplined, and properly clothed and bathed. However humble these tasks may be, they are good works in God's sight. A man also does good works when he runs his household well. Even if he did a hundred small tasks in a day, they would all be considered good if they were done in faith."[12] Again, this is to imply not that God has rigidly limited men and women to these roles but rather that He has set a structure in place that is the norm and ideal. And lest we think Luther did not hold women or his dear wife Katie in high regard, we should remember he also said things like, "A woman can do more with a child with one little finger than a man can with both fists."[13] Our modern denial of some sense of order of creation does not negate its reality.

So if the home is where the father ought to have the authority, over what does he exercise this authority? He has the authority to forgive and make new. It is where his authority is derived, not from his power, but from his grace. In his authority, the mother is set free to be mom. She cares, nurtures, guides, teaches, loves, entreats, and comforts her children. As Dr. Fairweather claims, "The structure of the emotionally healthy family is such that mother's authority is distinguished from father's authority not so much by its manifestation as such, but rather by how the mother relates and complements the father's authority. The basis in the mother's authority lies in how she relates to the father's authority—she affirms her own authority in affirming his. The polar concept gives a dynamic, depth quality to the experience of authority."[14]

In this way, the home is where we all encounter what Luther once termed "the mutual conversation and consolation of the brethren."[15] God's gracious goodness often comes to us in a way that we do not notice. He acts through people who are so common to us that we overlook how miraculously He is working through them. What is more common to us than our home and our father? But this is precisely why the father's actions in the home are so important. When Luther referred to this conversation, he elevated it to an almost sacramental level, as it has to do explicitly with the proclamation of the Gospel message. Says Luther,

> We will now return to the Gospel, which not merely in one way gives us counsel and aid against sin; for God is superabundantly rich [and liberal] in His grace [and goodness]. First, through the spoken Word by which the forgiveness of sins is preached [He commands to be preached] in the whole world; which is the peculiar office of the Gospel. Secondly, through Baptism. Thirdly, through the holy Sacrament of the Altar. Fourthly, through the power of the keys, and also through the mutual conversation and consolation of brethren, Matthew 18:20: "*Where two or three are gathered together, etc.*"[16]

Whether you know it or not, you have seen this happen. You have been this to your children in little ways that you probably don't even recognize. In fact, your forgiveness to your children hidden in the simple movements you make in the home every day has been a portion of God's superabundant grace.

The conversation in the home is the place (locus) of family fellowship, and the father is the caretaker of the conversation. It is a fellowship centered on giving and receiving as well as reaching out to one another and sharing the good news of forgiveness. It is easy for us to see this concept as too common. Can the forgiveness we receive in the home really be as powerful as God's forgiveness of the kind we receive at church? The conversations we have and we lead in the home as fathers may not always be "holy" as we understand it. Further, the gifts that we share with one another may seem wholly trivial. Our daily actions in the home may seem so trivial that we don't even consider them gifts. But if Luther is to be believed, these conversations both give and maintain us in God's rich grace. We are His means.

God had deigned to work through means. Thus we know that the Word and the Sacraments have the power, by the work of the Holy Spirit, to give faith and help the faithful persevere. God's richly proclaimed Word gives these gifts. We hear the Word in church, but our children first hear it in the home. From birth, they enter the conversation of the saints as they suckle their mother's breast and hear their father's voice. The home is where the father is free to make this seeming miracle an everyday occurrence and where he has the authority of his own voice to proclaim forgiveness.

### A Father's Home and Family

My daughter Amanda was about four years old. Ministry for me was busy and successful. Our church's youth ministry was growing by leaps and bounds. I had been spending many evening hours with teenagers doing what I loved. At home one evening, I asked Amanda to come and sit on my lap. She wouldn't. My wonderfully wise wife Terry later told me, "Greg, she doesn't know you." I was cut to the heart. I vowed that I would love nothing in this world more than my family. On vacation that summer, Amanda and I spent countless hours fishing and enjoying each other. One of my favorite pictures of all time is that precious golden-haired daughter holding up a string of rainbow trout that she had caught with a pole I had fashioned from an aspen tree. She had totally outfished her dad. I still choke up when I think about it. Recently, Amanda, newly married, put that picture on her Facebook page. Vacations with our family can be more important for a lifetime than we think.

After a vacation, people at church inevitably asked if I'm rested up and ready for ministry. I usually answer, "No, I'm totally worn out from having an awesome time with my wife and kids." I think God likes that answer.

When my son Adam was in first grade, Terry and I attended that spring's usual parent-teacher conference. When we met Adam's teacher, she looked concerned. As any parent, I thought, "Oh no, now what?" She asked us gravely what friend or relative had died. My wife and I looked at each other in total surprise.

I answered, "No one has died." "Oh," continued Adam's teacher, "he keeps talking about going to the cemetery." Terry and I laughed. Terry explained, "No, the Lord has led Greg to be a pastor, and this summer we're going to the . . . seminary." Be careful what you tell your kids; what they repeat can surprise you.

One summer our family vacationed at Pensacola Beach. Our youngest son, AJ, was about three years old. My wife and I, along with AJ, strolled down the Gulf seashore just after sunset. The sand was alive with movement. AJ reacted with understandable apprehension. All three of us got down on all fours to take a closer look. It was dozens of ghost crabs scurrying about. I grabbed one and we took a closer look. Ghost crabs are very small, but even those tiny claws can pinch. I found out the hard way. I cried out in pain, and we all laughed. Discovering the wonder of God's Creation can sometimes be painful, but you never know what can come from it. From that time on, AJ has loved searching for "creepy, crawly" things and has no apprehension picking them up, sometimes to his father's dismay.

Forrest Gump said, "Life is like a box of chocolates." I would add, "And our family is the gooey insides." Sometimes we like the flavor of our family, sometimes not, but our family always holds a surprise inside it. There's nothing sweeter than being a dad. Our Heavenly Father understands that.

Greg Rachuy, MDiv

## Conclusion

A father is thus a priest unto his family. He teaches and makes sacrifices, forgives and renews, all in the home. The home is then that first place where a child experiences God's goodness. God's love is a kairotic event, a crucial juncture, a moment of truth, the turning point. It is denotative in nature. You know God's love, but you don't "know" it in a way that is easily explained or systematized. You need the actual experience of it in order to truly know it. God provides fathers so that children can know His love in this denotative way. Fathers provide the opportunity for children to point at their dads and say, "God's love is like that. Like him over there. Like my dad." And the Christian home is where a dad does His work.

To where did the prodigal son return? He returned to his father's home. It was on the pathway to the father's home that the son was embraced by his father. It was in the portico of the father's home where servants were called to dress the sinner as a son. It was in the father's home where the dead son was made alive by the father's forgiveness. And it is in the father's home where we will all feast, rejoicing in the goodness of our Father. The father operates in his home. Thus my idea of heaven is the father's home.

We are a saved people, we are His children, we are redeemed, we are free, and we are a part of God's family. Let us not forget home and family and maybe even see it as that place wherein some of the paradoxes of this life are all at the same time revealed and solved. And in remembering, may the home be for you that place where you are free, the place that reminds you that your God is a God of love, warmth, and care on account of the freedom won for you in Christ. God's goodness to us by means of the home is what makes it such a sweet home. True homebuilding requires more than an exercise in human futility. In faith, we also humbly acknowledge, "Unless the Lord builds the house, those who build it labor in vain."[17]

CHAPTER 8

# A Healthy Reliance

*I, I am he who blots out your transgressions for my own sake, and I will not remember your sins.*

—Isaiah 43:25

As I write this chapter, I realize that, perhaps more than any other, it needs a disclaimer. So again, I am not any type of psychologist, nor do I claim to have any expertise in that field. I am a parent, associate dean, college professor, and theologian who is interested in the intersection between the theology of the Reformation and fatherhood. I am not an expert, just a thinker. Further, I think we have at one and the same time made our children, paradoxically, too reliant on us and yet not reliant enough.

## Gracious Reliance

Is there a difference between an unhealthy and a healthy reliance? As I have considered this topic, it has become clear to me that possessing a view of fathers such as I do—that is, that they are the models of grace in the home—creates in my children a reliance on me that seems endless and unbounded. This scares me. I am a considerable criticizer of helicopter and snowplow parents and wonder if that is the type of parent I am. I see in my kids, even the grown and married one, a deep reliance on me—and my wife, for that matter—and I wonder about the health of that reality and relationship.

I once had a conversation with Rod about this when I was a much younger man with much younger children. If I recall, he told me that he had received criticism from a friend saying that his children were too reliant on him, to which Rod retorted, "Maybe, but it's a healthy reliance." This in turn caused me to think, what does a healthy reliance from grown child to parent look like? In my position at the university, I see many parent–grown child relationships that seem unhealthy. I feel I could recognize this unhealthy reliance from a mile away, but a healthy one seems a little more vague to me.

Ironically, in my world this is a pretty hot topic. The last time I was together with our friends Paul and Cindy Koch, we discussed this same topic. How much reliance from grown child to parent is too much reliance? Perhaps the best approach is to break it down further and examine each situation. By utilizing a qualitative approach, comparing and contrasting unhealthy reliance versus healthy reliance may reveal the key differences.

From my observations, common behaviors are evident in an unhealthy reliance. First, when parents foster an unhealthy reliance, they appear to be afraid to allow their children to get hurt, experience loss, fail, or go through situations that are extremely difficult. Second, parents in this sort of relationship with their children reveal that they are afraid to say no for fear that their children will no longer love them. These same parents are willing to sacrifice everything while refusing to allow their grown children to sacrifice anything.[1] In turn, the grown children seem to see these sacrifices on the part of their parents as privileges to which they are entitled, perks of being lucky enough to be children of their parents.

A healthy reliance, on the other hand, is a giving relationship as well, but it is gracious, not smothering. A healthy reliance does not hide from the fact that children—even grown children—are sinners and will at times get hurt, experience loss, fail, and go through extremely difficult life situations. In turn, because a relationship of healthy reliance does not hide from this reality, parents will allow their children to experience those difficult aspects of living in a sinful and complex world. Because a healthy reliance is gracious, parents who employ this approach will not bring unyielding condemnation or sanctimony down on grown children when they experience failure; rather, they help them to pick up the pieces. Helping a child overcome adversity can be accomplished in many ways (I would not presume to know what is best for you or your family in any particular situation), but I would recommend that you always give the grown child the freedom to make the same damn mistakes all over again. The theme here is graciousness coupled with freedom. Parents are free to be gracious, and grown children are free to fail. There is no dictate.

How many times will grown children fail before we stop helping them? I'm not sure, but I am convinced that if their reliance is on our love for them, the grace that we show them, and the freedom with which we trust them, we are on the right track. If Rod is an example, and he has been for me, a healthy reliance is about grace, love, trust, freedom, and mercy. We Christians should already be familiar with these characteristics. Those of us who know that we are helpless sinners in need of a gracious Father to save us on account of His mercy shone on us in Christ will know that as parents, we have no greater example. We are shadows or imperfect reflections of His love for us, but we are shadows of this love nonetheless. We rely on His love for us as Christ proclaimed to us through the message of the Gospel. We rely on a message that is foolish, and from the outside looking in, that probably looks unhealthy. "For the word of the cross is folly to those who are perishing, but to us who are being saved it is the power of God."[2] Nevertheless, we couldn't dream of a healthier reliance. Our relationship with God is defined by our reliance on Him. In fact, this is why we go to His house, or church, to receive His good news and forgiveness.

## Absolution-Based Reliance

*Absolution* is the technical word that has been used in the church to signify the act of forgiving. My doktorvater (doctor father), James A. Nestingen, describes it this way: "There is a formal way of speaking the gospel in which the church has historically expressed its confidence: absolution. In the direct and personal declaration of the forgiveness of sin in Christ, the Gospel overlaps the law, both confirming its accusation and bringing the law to its end. Only sinners are forgiven; if you are forgiven, you must be one. Yet it is the very act of the absolution, with the freedom it brings, that allows the conclusion of repentance, 'I am a sinner,' to be drawn. Precisely where freedom dawns."[3]

Moreover, while the ritual practices of confession and absolution have fallen out of favor in many American Protestant settings, we still need to hear "You are free" in order to feel free. If you belong to a congregation that is lucky enough to have a pastor who preaches the Gospel, you will hear this on Sunday morning. If this is the case for you, rejoice; it is not the case for all. If you are a father, know that your children too need to hear a personal word of assurance and hope from your lips. I have said this already and will say it again: the Gospel comes to us on the lips of another. Forgiveness comes in conversations with your children. If they don't hear it from you, they'll seek this reassurance elsewhere.

In the current generation, some 41 percent of young people (ages eighteen to twenty-five) see a therapist at least once per week.[4] What are they looking for? I would say they are looking for the father's word of forgiveness and reassurance. Karl Augustus Menninger (1893–1990) was an American psychiatrist and a member of the Menninger family of psychiatrists who founded the Menninger Foundation and the Menninger Clinic in Topeka, Kansas. It is reported that Dr. Menninger said that some 70 or 80 percent of the people who want to talk to a counselor are looking for absolution.[5] It is a matter of uttering it, of taking courage in hand and actually speaking the word of pardon in Christ's name. A healthy reliance means that your children know where they are safe. They know that it is with you, their father, protector, and forgiver, where they find pardon and peace in the home.

The reliance a father provides is one that is based on absolution. What our children need from us is support and forgiveness. Absolution, or forgiveness of sins, is what we seek from the church, or at least ought to receive from it. I have said many times that this book is examining the life of fatherhood through a narrow lens. My goal is not to provide the whole scope of fatherhood in practice. Rather, my goal is to examine the theological connection between a father and his children and how that relates to our relationship as children of the Heavenly Father.

Absolution then is not something that overlooks all the sins and the faults of the sinner. Rather, absolution provides forgiveness for those sins. A father who absolves creates reliance in his children precisely because they need to be forgiven. He knows their sins. He knows their faults. He is intimately aware of every sinful shortcoming they are trying to hide. Yet he absolves, washes away, forgives, and makes new on account of Christ. This need for forgiveness will always create reliance between father and child. Some fathers will forgive, and some will not. Those forgiving fathers, I think, will discover that their children will be able to find their way home, much like in the parable.

All of us who are bold enough to call ourselves Christian feel this reliance deep inside us. We know that God knows our inward thoughts. We know that He knows we are unclean. We know that if we rely on Him alone and the salvation He has won for us through Christ, we will be saved. We also know that we need to hear the voice of absolution; His voice calling us home.

But what about repentance? Is a father to forgive without demanding a sincere apology? I often rely on the words of my mentor, Dad Rod, when it comes to repentance: "All our repentance is half-assed." It is imperative that fathers know that repentance is not a prerequisite for absolution; rather, it is a consequence of the Gospel. In one sense, there is a conditionality attached. There is no faith without repentance, just as there is no repentance without faith. We repent because of our faith in the Father's forgiveness. Yet even if we do not say the words, are we not still forgiven? The power of repentance lies not in the words spoken by the sinner but in the words spoken by Christ: "You are forgiven in my name." Thus the words of the father to his children, "You are forgiven," echo and shadow the words of our Lord. True repentance is more accurately described by the prayer of Augustine: "Give what you command, and command what you will."[6] The Lord always gives what He commands, and thus we rely on Him for all. This is a healthy reliance because it clings to forgiveness and salvation. Oh how great is it that we as mere earthly dads can mirror this great gift in some little way to our children.

## Unspoken Forgiveness, No Confession Needed

There once was a young man whose father was dying. This young man had not been a good son. In his youth, he was disobedient. In his teenage years, he had caused his father many sleepless nights. He even wrecked the family car once in a drunken bender with his buddies. While in college, he rarely called his parents, he seemed annoyed at their presence during family weekends, and yet he expected the timely receipt of the tuition check every year and his allowance every month. The same was mostly true while he was completing his graduate work; he was too focused on success to bother with his mother or father. Once the young man was in his career, he threw himself into the life of a young professional with the zeal of a new convert. He worked endless hours, never seeming to have time for his father—or anyone else, really. Then the man got married and had his own family, and he still did little to wrap his two worlds together, leaving his own mother and father at an arm's distance.

Over the many years, the man had thought about changing the situation and apologizing to his father. Yet he always put off discussing with his dad how important he was to him, how he loved him, and how grateful he was to him. Then one day, he got a call from his mother saying that his dad was dying, and it wouldn't be long. So when the man jumped in the car and began the thousand-mile trek home, like the prodigal son, he rehearsed his apology, his confession, all the way home. What would he say to his dad after all these years?

As he rehearsed, he knew it wouldn't be easy to apologize for all the "bad things" that he had done. What he felt was inexcusable were his loveless actions throughout the years. It was not the overt sin that caused him the most guilt but rather the omissions of love and appreciation throughout his life. So he went home, did what he could, helped his mother, and waited for the right opportunity to really talk to his dad.

One day, they were driving to one of his father's final doctor appointments when the man finally got up the courage to speak. As the man opened his mouth, tears streamed down his face, and the quivering of voice was unmistakable. The man coyly said to his father, "Dad, I am sorry for how I have hurt you all these years."

The man didn't really know what to expect, as he was somewhat unaccustomed to making confessions of this type. He had never even really apologized to his wife after a fight. Maybe he thought his dad would have said, "Well, it is about damned time!"

At least then he could have felt like he'd gotten through to his dad. But instead the father just looked out the window and asked his son if he thought it was going to rain. Astounded by the lack of response, and thinking maybe the sickness was affecting his father's hearing, he tried his confession again. "Dad," said the son, "did you hear me? I want you to know that I am sorry for being so awful to you all these years." Again, the man's father seemed untouched. Rather, the father simply glanced lovingly at his son and said, "Welcome home."

Just a few weeks later, his father died. After the funeral reception, as he was helping his mother clean up, the man asked his mother about the attempts at an apology he had made to his father. He told her it was like it didn't even faze his dad at all and as if all the years of neglect meant nothing. His mother acknowledged that she and his father had discussed the man's apology before his death. "He told me you apologized," she said, "and he told me he was so happy that you found your way home." His mom continued, "He didn't know what else to say; in his mind, you were always forgiven."

All the years of neglect, thoughtlessness, and scornful maleficence meant nothing compared to the reality that the son had finally returned. The thoughtlessness and neglect be damned, the father had forgotten all of it. "For my son was dead, and now he is alive. He was lost and now is found."[7]

Sometimes it requires an apology to our earthly fathers to cast the reflection where we then see our Heavenly Father's forgiveness in our own father's forgetfulness. Of course, being repentant is part of the new life we now live in Christ, but it is not our penitence that brings forgiveness. Rather, it is the father's love and favor on account of Christ that brings about our forgiveness. Before we are even done confessing, we are forgiven; He will remember our sins no more. When a good dad forgets the sins of his children, it assures them that their sins against their Heavenly Father are also forgotten on account of Christ. Like the father of the prodigal son, like the father in this story, like good dads everywhere, our Father welcomes us back. He stands looking down the road waiting for our return. Before we can even make it all the way home, He rushes out to meet us and says, "Welcome home."

### Eulogy for My Father

I'm going to make an attempt to talk about three things my dad did for me that I believe were absolutely spot on. Indian Guides (similar to Boy Scouts) was one of those things. My dad set it up—I wasn't even sure I wanted to be involved. My dad knew better. Some of my finest memories are sitting around an oil drum fire pit (when parks still allowed that sort of thing) and warming my hands from the cold while we talked about the world and my place in it—a place that he had given me. In Indian Guides, he taught me how to run and fight and fish . . . and just *be* with other men.

Working on stuff with my dad was always a treat. It didn't matter what it was; we would always wind up arguing with each other about whatever we were working on and ultimately wind up distressing the women. It was men using their anger to get something done even if it caused an injury, which it usually did. While my dad attended to his injured fingers, we would admire the completed project, whether it was the carburetor on my orange '71 Pinto or a brake cylinder on his Chevy Malibu, and marvel at how we had made it through this battle with our meager skills.

One of the other projects was the soapbox derby racer. We spent time on it and did everything we could on that little, blue, wooden car. I didn't win any prizes or anything, but it made a good showing. The most important thing was that he instigated the whole project, and I was kind of "swept up" in it. He knew what I wanted even though I didn't: that time with him, with him showing me *how* and showing me the way to get something done with a lot of screaming and mismeasurements and detours. I was really happy just joyously hollering with him at the disobedient tools that tried to thwart my participation in the race.

Math was not my dad's strong suit—nor is it mine. I was failing algebra my sophomore year in high school. When my dad got wind of it from the teacher, he started helping me. I was sitting at the kitchen table staring uncomprehendingly at a problem. My dad leaned over me and fought me for the book. While he leaned over, trapping me there, he turned back to the first page in the chapter and began to read. It seemed as though an eternity went by. When he had finished reading, he had me write out the solution to the first problem, dictating every number to me. Then he explained the formulas involved and worked with me for hours until I got it. He went through this identical process every school night for an entire year. He never lost his patience with me. He never made me feel stupid. He showed me how to study. He showed me what patience was, and I think I owe a good chunk of what little I have of it to our math study sessions in 1982.

To the man who raised me, taught me how to be a good Indian, helped me succeed at algebra, and helped me build a soapbox derby racer. To Joseph Byrnes, my father: "Catch you later, babe."

Steve Byrnes, MA

## A Tale of Two Fathers

A healthy reliance is about finding one's way home, even when home is no longer a place to go but rather a moment of forgiveness and support. I have a good friend who has been a college professor for fifteen years. Just for fun, I'll call him Professor X. He and I are roughly the same age, though he finished graduate school quickly and has been in higher education since his midtwenties. He recently told me a story that not only brought me to tears; it reminded me of how dependent children really are on their father's forgiveness and support. He recounted that teaching undergraduate theology has changed over the last fifteen years. When he started out, he claims that it was easier in one simple way: most of his students were the children of Christians who laid a rather heavy law trip on their kids. These young adults felt the weight of their sins—sins clearly identified by the traditional evangelical churches—and they had an acute awareness of their own shortcomings. Professor X recounted that sin was about their personal moral failings. In such a setting, he found little trouble teaching the classic Reformation teachings about the distinction and interplay between Law and Gospel, and he said that it was like pointing out an oasis in the desert.

More recently, Professor X has become aware of the reality that his students are much more diverse. He notes that he averages a couple Muslim students in each class, several nonreligious students from China, and a healthy dose of secularized suburban Anglo students. Further, he told me something of which anyone who teaches in the modern university is keenly aware: modern students tend to fear only one judgment, that of failing to live up to the expectations of their heavily involved and constantly hovering parents. This is all the more acute when it comes to international students whose families are banking everything on their success.

This past year, he has gotten to know two international students well. One is from South Africa and the other is from an uncompromisingly Muslim country in the Middle East. When his South African student converted to Christianity, her father gathered her extended family and surrounding village for a ceremony to "celebrate" her new faith. They sacrificed a goat and declared that she was no longer a daughter of the father. She was told that the gods and ancestral spirits no longer would offer protection for her but rather a curse. She was cast off and despised. Professor X recounted to me that this was the first time that the passage from Luke 14:26 ever really made sense to him: "If anyone comes to me and does not hate his own father and mother and wife and children and brothers and sisters, yes, and even his own life, he cannot be my disciple." As he explained it, I too began to comprehend that it was a verse that any young person from a traditional society could understand: to change one's religious beliefs is not merely a personal decision, as it is to most Americans; it was an affront to the beliefs of generations of forebears. Jesus, master of hyperbole and artful spiritual rhetoric, didn't want her to actually hate her father, of course; Jesus was giving permission to a new disciple to step out in faith, even when it cost the loss of family connections. She joined a vast new family that gave her confidence and hope enough to go back to a hostile father and offer blessings where there were parental curses. Professor X told me that at least for this young woman, this love in the face of anger has had a profoundly positive effect on her siblings. Also, they expected her to fail because of the curse, but her siblings have seen her accomplishments and success. Further, her dad is at least still connected enough to accept money from the young woman as she works several jobs in the United States.

As tears welled up in his eyes, Professor X said, "Then there's my delightful student from the Middle East." He continued to explain that after several years of studying Christianity and seriously wrestling with her personal beliefs, she asked for a very public baptism. At this point, all he could tell me was that he wept. Growing up in American Christianity, he, like so many of us in his experience, had never seen a testimony to faith as sincere as this young woman's was. I was there the day of her baptism, and I understand it when he says, "I'll never again recite the creed without remembering the tearful confession of this student as she stood before the baptismal font." And Professor X, as well as every educated person who was in the little chapel that day, knows that with this sacrament, she closed a door to family and put her own safety in danger in a way most Western students can hardly imagine.

Professor X says that she told her mother immediately, but her father didn't learn of her baptism until weeks later. When he did, he called. "You can never, never come home again," he said. Never come home? Immediately, images of her room, things, friends, and siblings flashed before her. Never again would these familiar things be intimately close to her; they would have to be a world away. Most of us who know even very little about her culture expected that this was how things might go, but the rest of the story was entirely unexpected. Again, the tears could not be stopped from running down his cheeks, and his voice quivered as this stalwart professor told me the rest of the tale as it was told to him by this faithful new sister. "Are you going to cut off my funding for the university?" She asked. "No," the father responded, "I love you so much, and I have done everything in my power to keep you safe and happy. If you were to come home, I might have to watch my countrymen harm you, and there would be nothing I could do to stop it. I will continue to pay for your education, and, what's more, hire you a top attorney to help you gain asylum." "Are you mad that I became a Christian?" After a poignant pause, he said, "I love you more than anything in this world. You are one of the smartest young women I know, and though I have never learned about this Jesus, you have had a long time to study his teachings. So I can only trust that you made a wise and sincere decision. So I support you." Professor X and the girl cried for a while in his office after she told him. He begged her to make sure that she told her dad what a wonderful example of a father he is. Indeed, along with Professor X, I think we all wonder if we could put that much trust in our bright and virtuous children.

The best fathers are those who are able, in special moments like this, to oppose all societal impulses to hate a beloved child and help them find their way home, even when they can never come home. The best fathers provide astounding grace and love, even when they don't understand the reasons their children make the decisions they do. They respect the adulthood of their young adults. In our affluent and comfortable culture, we often hear of parents who disown their children for switching majors, taking a job in another state, or marrying a starving artist. We parents spend the first half of our kids' lives helping them make the right decisions. We spend the rest of their lives, after adulthood, learning to let them seek lives of integrity with the virtues we've tried to instill in them and learning to actually love at the true risk of the loss of their love. But if we want to maintain astounding grace and love, we have to let go like that brave father who did all he could to make sure his beloved daughter never came home.

## The Prodigal Son Absolved

Things don't work out for the prodigal the way any of us expected it to. What does happen to him makes no sense from any perspective. It is probably not possible in any parable or story to completely capture the mystery of what it means to be saved by God in Christ. Yet in this tale, we have some inkling of what it might mean. The father is in the house; it is always safe to come home. The son, as he was stuck in the mire of all his guilt, is sure of only one thing. He said, "How many of my father's hired servants have more than enough bread, but I perish here with hunger! I will arise and go to my father."[8] He can rely on his father. It is safe to go home. He, like the young man in the earlier story, had his confession all planned out. "'I will say to him, Father, I have sinned against heaven and before you. I am no longer worthy to be called your son. Treat me as one of your hired servants.' And he arose and came to his father."[9]

The father does not require of the son a protracted confession of guilt, because it is always safe to come home. The father merely absolves before the confession can even fully leave his lips.

But while he was still a long way off, his father saw him and felt compassion, and ran and embraced him and kissed him. And the son said to him, "Father, I have sinned against heaven and before you. I am no longer worthy to be called your son." But the father said to his servants, "Bring quickly the best robe, and put it on him, and put a ring on his hand, and shoes on his feet. And bring the fattened calf and kill it, and let us eat and celebrate. For this my son was dead, and is alive again; he was lost, and is found."[10]

You can always come home. The calf has been killed, and thus the celebration that is the Father's house must begin. My words of forgiveness will always be free to you. Our kids rely on our strong word of grace to point them to the Father. They ought to feel that they can rely on us, in a healthy way, just as we rely on our Heavenly Father. Our words to them are echoes of the Word of Life. God has placed us in their lives to be just that: faith, hope, and love on the lips of another. You can rely on that.

# CHAPTER 9
# Stories of and from Fathers

I have spent a good amount of time in this book describing what types of events can be created in order to provide a sense of magical deliverance in the lives of children. As I concluded my writing, I thought it would be helpful to provide stories of and from fathers sharing events that actually happened that were Christocentrically apologetic in character. I would like to thank all those friends and family who contributed to this portion of the book. You have all, in some way or another, at some time or another, served as a little Christ to me.

Jonathan Ruehs, MA, MA, Th
Associate Pastor, Outreach, Concordia University Irvine

One very strong memory from my days of adolescence is the time my dad took me out to the middle of the desert to teach me how to shoot a real rifle. I grew up shooting a BB gun in the backyard of my Phoenix suburban home (no I didn't shoot my eye out; my dad taught me that you don't shoot a BB gun at an aluminum sign because it will bounce back at you), and so at the very least I knew how to handle a weapon, even a weak one. Yet I had never had the chance to shoot the 16-gauge shotgun that sat high up in my father's closet, a remnant from his own childhood days growing up in rural Michigan. I recall it was in late September of my freshman year when we went on our shooting excursion. It was around midmorning on a Saturday that we loaded up the 16-gauge, my brother Todd's .22, a big garbage bag full of cans, and a couple of industrial-sized plastic buckets filled with water. Back in those days, a quick thirty-minute drive brought you to the outskirts of northern Phoenix, where you could drive your car down some dirt road into the middle of nowhere to shoot guns. When we got to where we were going, we set up our shooting gallery. My dad first started teaching me how to shoot the .22, and after some basic instructions, I was pinging cans off our makeshift shooting range. He then showed me how to fire the 16-gauge. He showed me how to keep the butt of the rifle tight against my shoulder in order to minimize the buck from the gun. I recall aiming the rifle at one of the full buckets of water, and when I pulled back the trigger, the blast from the gun shattered the bucket into hundreds of pieces. My dad and I laughed and cheered at the destruction that we wrought with his own childhood rifle. We probably spent about an hour out there in the desert destroying cans and buckets. It was the only time that my dad and I went out to the desert to shoot, but it is a memory that I cherish. I cherish it because it was a difficult time for me as I was transitioning into high school, which was a place that was just as unfamiliar as the faces that I saw in those halls day after day, students whom I had not gone to junior high with but many of whom had been in middle school together. It was important for that young, pimply faced teen to find an anchor of familiarity in the midst of that adolescent chaos. My dad, those guns, and that Saturday was that anchor.

Paul Koch, MDiv
Grace Lutheran Church, Ventura, California

*The Haircut*

Today is haircut day for my son. Now, usually, I just break out the clippers and cut his hair myself, but I have to tell you, there is great joy in taking him to my barber and having his hair done by a man that knows what he is doing. Just about now, it's time to drive down to the barbershop where the language is a little foul and people are just as content to sit around and join the conversation as they are to get their hair cut. There is a beauty to the barbershop that I can't quite describe, and I love that I get to experience it with my son.

The barber sets him up on the booster seat; other than that one piece of furniture, he is treated like any other man in the joint. Now, being only four years old, it is a lot of work for Titus to sit still for that long. He manages quite well as he is engulfed in adult conversation, either being the butt of the jokes or being asked to help make fun of the guys cutting hair next to him. It's good for him to experience this, to soak in the atmosphere, even if he is just thinking about the ice cream I promised him afterward.

As I look at my son, I am filled with pride and hopefulness. I might well fear for a boy growing up in a world that has embraced the role of men as narcissistic metrosexuals or overly trendy hipsters. But I don't. Much of what passes for manhood these days holds no sway over the character of a true man, and the shaping of that character lies not in the whims of a consumerist society but in the actions and words of his father.

I have five children, and my son is the youngest. That's right, he has four older sisters! While he has certainly learned how to use them and their motherly instincts to his advantage, he has also learned about restraint and patience. He has learned that you can't hit a girl, no matter how much they might deserve it. He has learned the importance of holding open the door to the ladies of the house before entering himself. He has watched me love and care for his mother and all his sisters; while I have certainly made many mistakes, he is still learning to be a man.

You see, I believe that I am the single biggest influence upon my son's life. The man he will become, his character and resolve, will be a byproduct of my own character: my own interactions with those around us, my own treatment of those who need caring for, who need welcome, who need forgiveness. I'm saying that I expect my son to be a man of integrity and resolve. I expect him to interact with this world and hold his own. I expect him to treat his future wife with honor and respect. And as silly as it may sound, sometimes that begins with a trip to the barbershop to practice the things of manhood and to come home with our heads held high and our bellies full of ice cream!

## The Awesomest

As a father of five, you might think that I am more of a wreck than I let on—or at least that I should be. Of course, there is the constant desire for that elusive thing called a "quiet house" or my fleeting hope to be able to take the family out to eat for under a hundred bucks (even as I endure the strange looks on the hostess's face as she pushes two tables together for *all* my kids). But beyond that, there is a relentless flow of heartbreaking news that pours into our lives, placing great stress on my family and preying upon my fears as a father.

The twenty-four-hour news cycles and constant updates via the interweb allow unfettered access to all the brutal and ugly things of our world. These things ought to make me worried about the future of my children. With the terror of Christians being beheaded by ISIS still in our memories, we turn the channel only to be faced with the riots in Baltimore. We turn off the television and open our computers to be greeted with the horrific news of a discovery of a newborn baby's body parts found in LA County. Then with all these images floating around my head, I sit down to dinner with my family. There, five young and (mostly) ignorant faces join my wife and me in prayer, unfazed by the insanity of it all. When I look at them, I ought to weep. I ought to be consumed with worry. I ought to be a complete wreck.

But on this day, my five-year-old son says to me with all the confidence in the world, "Dad, you're the awesomest!"

Now that may just sound like a funny thing a kid says about his dad. It might simply bring a smile to the face of every father who sips his coffee out of a "#1 Dad" mug. But those words are a subtle (or perhaps not-so-subtle) reminder of the power of fatherhood. As I sit down to dinner with my family gathered around me, I'm not just a helpless victim of a broken world. I don't have to watch powerless as my children are tossed to the wolves. I'm a dad, and that is no small thing!

By design, I have far greater influence on my children than the terrors of this world.

I can deliver strength, safety, and assurance within the home that is unmatched in our society. I can inspire revolution and obstinate resistance to the ways of our culture in the delightful anarchy of my family. In fact, even the Law and the Gospel are products of my words and actions long before my children learn them in church.

The problem is that we are quick to forget this power of fatherhood. We are soon convinced by the relentless shouts of the world and the many portrayals of fathers as impotent and bumbling fools so that we begin our retreat. It's not that we want to concede the field, but the deck seems stacked against us. This retreat from our position and vocation is aided by two things above all else: our own broken-ness and the silence of our children.

Notice, it was my five-year-old son that said I was the awesom-est and not my fifteen-year-old daughter. It's not that she wouldn't say it, but it certainly doesn't flow as effortlessly as it did when she was little. As our children grow, they also begin to trust the nar-rative the world tells. Just as they no longer believe in the magic of their childhood when scientific explanation replaces the wonder and awe of nature, so too the magic of their father's power and love can be shaken by the disturbing realities of our culture. They also hear the cries to look elsewhere for strength and protection. They become aware of the failures of fathers. They quit reminding us of our power, for they begin to doubt it.

This abridged reminder from the lips of our children is comple-mented by our own brokenness. As we struggle with sin, as we fail over and over again with the same old temptations and perversions, we begin to think that their hushed voices are warranted. How can a man like me, a man full of doubts and fears, a man who fails more than I would ever let on, a man that feels small and helpless in the face of such opposition, how can I actually change things? What can I really do in the face of such atrocities? But then again, I am a dad.

I can shape the vision of what sort of husband my daughters will desire more than any television show. I can show them day in and day out how a man should treat a woman. I can protect and guide better than any other force in their lives. I can teach my son more about strength and fear than the nightly news. He can learn more than kneejerk consumerism and dead-end nihilism. He can learn honor, friendship, and compassion from me.

And here's the thing: we fathers can be this powerful force in the face of our own brokenness despite the depravity of our souls. For though our world drowns out the voices of our children, though our sin is clearly reflected in the Law, we live in the love of our Father. It is a love that forgives and makes whole. It is a love that doesn't just say, "It's all right," but actually does something about it. A love that was born, suffered, died, and rose so that you might die and rise to new life. And so you are new! You are fathers bearing the love of the

Father, and the world cannot stop such love. "Faith, hope, and love abide, these three; but the greatest of these is love."[1]

To put it simply, you are the awesomest!

## Cindy Koch, MA
### Wife and Mother of Five

*Wait 'til Your Father Gets Home*

My childhood memories of my father are not complete. I can only remember certain days, certain places, certain things that we did together. My sister and I recently talked about our memories and tried to fill in the blanks for each other. We remembered little things like ice cream trips, putting gas in the car, bike rides, and board games. It seems as if there was a lifetime of things that we have forgotten now that we moved into our own world of husband, kids, and adult life.

My father traveled when I was a girl, and I'm told that he was often gone. But when I think about my dad, I can remember the times when he was at home. Truth be told, I learned the character of my dad from a very young age. When I would be less than an angel for my mom (and that was very often), I remember looking forward to those words, "Wait 'til your father gets home." It did not hold the terror and fear of punishment. In my experience, my mother had exhausted every good discipline technique she ever learned, and she had no more energy to deal with me. My father brought patience and a calm resolution.

I was so cared for by my father that I came to expect this gracious and loving attitude from all men. As I stretched my wings away from the safe nest of home, boys came and went. Without even knowing it, I was always measuring them up to my dad. When a boy was dishonest and broke my heart, I knew somehow this was not right. Men were supposed to love and care for women. When a boy tried to quickly move a relationship in the physical direction, I was bold enough to want something more. I could always look back to the anchor that was my father, one who would take care of me.

In college, I had an amazing professor, Dr. Rosenbladt, and he helped me realize what treasure my dad had given me. The theological students at Concordia University flocked to this particular man because of his unashamed teaching of the freedom of the Gospel. They loved this man because he cared for them and their education. He did not hold the rules over their heads; rather, he broke the rules for their sake. I remember a moment of teary panic when my car had a flat tire and this man patiently looked at me and calmly explained that he was going to take care of it. That's when it hit me: Dr. Rosenbladt was my father!

The loving mercy that both he and my father have shown to me is not just a strange coincidence. They reflect the compassion that we dare to expect from our Father in Heaven. I was fortunate enough to have been given an earthly father who taught me. Not everyone has this, but God does not leave his children alone. The patience and kindness of God is given to us through Christ. Christ's words are spoken on the lips of men like Dr. Rosenbladt and my father. I am forgiven, I am comforted, and I can't wait until my Father comes home for good.

Bob Hiller, MDiv
Faith Lutheran Church Moorpark

*Father Knows Best*

As I view the cultural landscape, I am troubled by how readily we thumb our noses at dear old dad. We have gone from an overly idealized "father knows best" to soft-in-the-middle, bumbling Ray Barone in the matter of a generation. Through cultural icons such as Papa of the Berenstain Bears, the feminization of America has demoted dad to nothing more than that sports-watching, beer-drinking, lazy waste of space that lives in front of the television and requires mom's mothering to survive. But fathers are gifts from the Lord. In fact, no one has a greater impact on how we view the world, family, church, and especially God than those men who hold the place of "father" in our lives. We need to fight against the trends that belittle fatherhood and encourage fathers to be strong, kind, and wise leaders in their homes, men who fight for their brides and provide for their children and who take responsibility for their families and are not afraid of offending those who get in their way. We need more men like my dad.

Since going to seminary, I've learned that balancing home and church is hard for many pastors. I didn't learn that from my dad. He was home for nearly every dinner, even when he had meetings. He made virtually all our games; when he couldn't, it was because of an emergency. My dad knew the difference between spending time with his bride and Christ's bride. From where I sat, I never saw the latter create jealousy in the heart of the former. He was home for his family, and we knew we were his priority.

Don't get me wrong, he isn't a lazy pastor. He loves the church. He made sure we did too. It wasn't until two years ago that I realized my Sunday morning routine is almost identical to my dad's. He used to wake me up early on Sundays so I could tag along as he prepared for the service. I watched as he opened the doors, turned on the lights, and made sure the sanctuary was in order for God's Word to invade the lives God's people. After telling me to leave the sanctuary so he could run through his sermon, I would peek through the window to spy on his routine. Now when I preach, especially when proclaiming the gospel, I can actually hear my father's voice come out of my mouth.

I'm Lutheran because my dad taught me to listen to the scriptures alone. The poor man was burdened with a family who loved to argue theology. (We still do, in fact. He suffers sermon critiques every time my brother, who will soon have a doctorate in theology from University of Chicago, and pain-in-the-rear me come home for Christmas.) One of my favorite memories is sitting down for Sunday lunch and my mom saying, "What right do we have to 'give God glory'? We can't give him anything! Why do we say it?" My dad coolly replied, "It's in the Bible. We didn't make it up. We don't correct the Bible."

Or when I went through a theologically "rebellious" phase in college, I called home to tell my parents that I was leaving the Lutheran Church and joining the Reformed Baptists. After all, they got baptism right. I came out to my mom first. She listened patiently, as she always does. She told me she'd tell dad to call me when he got home. Then she called dad immediately, as she always does. He called me within five minutes. Not being a phone guy, this was no small move. "So your mom says you aren't Lutheran anymore." "Yeah, I just don't think it is what the Bible teaches, especially on baptism." I made my case. I'll never forget his words: "Well . . . open your Bible." So now I'm a Lutheran pastor, not because my dad is one, but because my dad taught me to read the Bible.

Fathers, more than anyone, shape how we view God. My dad gave me a gracious picture of God. My dad is far from perfect. He has his faults. I know them well as I see them in my own life from time to time. But he was there. He loves his family. He trained up his boys in the way they should go. He gave us a nostalgic love for baseball and an appetite for good theology. Most importantly, he gave us Christ. I know we all want to go to heaven and have all our questions answered. But I sometimes find myself hoping that it isn't true. A heaven where I grab a beer with my dad, my brother, and my kids and argue theology around an Angel's game wouldn't be so bad.

## Joshua Theodore Keith

### *Spider-Man versus the Rhino*

I have many wonderful memories of the magic my father created throughout my childhood: BMX and mountain biking, building Legos Star Wars sets, watching movies and shows that I was probably a little too young for. Out of all the great memories and experiences I had with my father, probably the best and earliest memories I have are wrestling.

Now when I say wrestling, I'm not talking about the sport where men in spandex straddle each other or about what the Rock is cooking. I'm talking about racing to my parents' bedroom, throwing all the pillows and blanket off the mattress, and tackling my dad futilely, only to be picked up and thrown back down onto the bed, giggling all the while. The only rule was if you were the first to fall off the bed, you lost. I remember doing this a lot throughout my childhood, and I remember the recurring theme of our brawls being that I would pretend to be Spider-Man and my dad would be the Rhino (which if you didn't know is a villain in the Spider-Man comics).

I grew up in the early 2000s, and Marvel had just started premiering their iconic superhero movies, one of which featured my favorite superhero, Spider-Man. After watching the movies, reading the comics, and playing the video games of the friendly neighborhood web slinger, who in their five- to ten-year-old mind didn't want to be Spider-Man? But none of the previously mentioned games, movies, or comics brought nearly as much magic to being a superhero as going against the Rhino (my father) on the streets of Manhattan (the bed). He made what seemed impossible—things that couldn't possibly exist outside of what was make-believe—real to me.

As I grew older, we started wrestling less, but the magic that it brought never actually ended. Wrestling grew into lightsaber fights, where we would swing wildly at each other with sticks of plastic until one of us howled with pain from getting smacked on the fingers. This led into Nerf gun shootouts, which usually ended in arguments with my brother sounding a bit like this: "Hey! I totally just shot you, you're dead," which inevitably would lead to the response, "Nuh huh, the bullet only hit my shirt!" And things only got better when I was thirteen. One day, my best friend, Noah, and I started making wooden weapons and shields. Oh, the look on my mother's face when we would come in from pretty much beating each other to a sweaty, bruised, bloody pulp, and then to look over and see my dad sitting in a chair with a smile that said, "My boy."

Though I don't get to do these things very much anymore, my father still manages to make me feel like a superhero. I'm currently eighteen, and I'm a young man who finds joy in working with his hands, a fleeting passion nowadays. I work a nine-to-five job at a cabinet shop and come home every evening for dinner feeling exhausted, but at the same time I feel amazing, and I've never gone to bed feeling better than on a day when I've worked hard. Even though this might be thought of as an unpopular or "lower-class" way of working, it's what I enjoy doing. I've never felt happier or felt that I'm doing the right thing to follow my calling than when my dad tells me he's proud of the man I've become or when I get home from a long day of work and see my dad with a smile that says, "That's my boy!"

## Autumn Whitney Grace Keith

### Leprechauns

For most of my childhood, my dad worked as the director of the after school program at our local community center. Before I was old enough to join my brothers at the town's Lutheran elementary school, I would go with my dad and hang out in the prekindergarten room while my mom worked nights as either a waitress or as a unit clerk at the local hospital. The prekindergarten room was right across the gymnasium from my dad's office. I thought it was the most amazing thing to be able to wave to him from wherever I was in the building.

The prekindergarten teacher was Ms. Rhonda, who I would like to add to my long list of important influences of my childhood. She taught me many useful things such as not to sit "criss-cross applesauce" when wearing a skirt and also that leprechauns are most certainly real. Leprechauns tend to show up around Saint Patrick's Day. In preparation, my class made traps out of shoeboxes filled with foil and colored with shamrocks, glitter, and all kinds of things that would attract these greedy little creatures. Ms. Rhonda also put pie tins of paint in front of all the doors so we could track the tiny footprints if and when they came.

As kids, my brothers and I never believed in Santa, the Tooth Fairy, the Easter Bunny, or any of the usual hubbub parents tell their children. We knew our parents bought our presents at Christmas and we dyed our own eggs before Easter and painted Jesus on it, so who needed a bunny? We never felt deprived without these creatures, but there was one species of magical fauna I was sure just couldn't be fake: Leprechauns. I told my brothers this, and they tried with all their might to convince me of how silly I sounded and how illogical I was being, but six-year-old me wouldn't budge. My dad quickly intervened and told my brothers to let me have fun with my only imaginary friend, Lenny Leprechaun. That was the first time I can recall when my dad stood with me and my fascination with my favorite magical people.

As was not completely uncommon for me at this age, I became sick to the point of missing class one day. But this was no ordinary class I was going to miss: to me, this was the most important class ever, the one where we check the traps for leprechauns! Aside from being pitiful with sickness, I was heartbroken at the thought of not seeing the traps or footprints. Seeing my forlorn frame, my father did the best thing in the world he could have ever done for me: he took me to the community center—all sick and pitiful—and carried me in. He unlocked the door with his magical skeleton key and took me in to check my shoebox trap. I remember feeling so sick that I couldn't even walk and then so elated at seeing the rainbow of tiny footprints littering the ground! My box lid hadn't yet fallen, but others had, and

I knew what that must have meant. The leprechauns had been there, and the magic was most certainly real for me that day.

This story might not seem like it would mean that much, but to me at six years old, it was the most magical thing. All hope of being at what seemed the most important event of my life was lost, but then my hero delivered me from my sadness, my father, sweeping in and saving the day! This memory has been forever ingrained into my mind and brings tears to my eyes even today. The substance of this variation of magic was what made this story so utterly extraordinary. My father has taken my brothers and me on much more extravagant adventures, but when asked to write a story of my dad's magic in my life, this story sticks out. It showed me how much he cared about even my smallest of desires, and he strove to make my wishes come true—and still does.

## Money for Books

Even this week, my father stepped in and showed me how much he cares for me. Shopping with Mum today, I spent some of my hard-earned babysitting money on my favorite thing in the world: books. I spent $120.68 on six precious volumes but had only $85.00 on my person. I made a deal with my mother that she would pay the rest of the money I didn't have, but we would transfer the money from my bank account when we got home. This transaction of the remaining money had to be made from Pa's phone. When told he had to transfer the money, he tried to get Mum not to split hairs and just let it go, but she was firm on this point. After being unable to persuade her to release the debt, he took it upon himself and gave up $35.00 of his seldom-acquired cash and freed me from my burden.

This isn't a story about how much of a bitch Mum is or anything like that. She was completely justified in her pursuit of my debt. It's not like I couldn't afford it or didn't have enough money in my account, and I hadn't even asked her to help me out or carry the cost (which if I had, I'm sure she would have readily done). Pa knows I could afford it and that I would pay it, but he didn't want me to have to. He loves me and is willing to do anything for me, even the smallest debt he is completely willing to take upon himself and show his grace to me. As

I write, I'm brought to tears and filled with the struggle of trying to express to you, the reader, how much this act of deliverance means to me. In short, I don't know what I would do without my father, and I can think of no better example of God's grace than the earthly father who tries in every aspect of his life to pour down on his children the living example of grace.

## Rev. Graham Glover

### *The Worst and the Best Seventy-Two Hours of My Life*

My daughter turned ten today. Like all parents, I will never forget the day she was born. Our first child, her birth was, at that point, the single best day of my life (I say this with all due apologies to my wife and our glorious wedding day, but I think she agrees with me).

I was simply overwhelmed when our daughter was born. As is the case with many first-time parents, I was elated, even if a bit frightened about what being a father is all about. Holding her for the first time, I remember saying to myself, "Am I really a father?!" The emotions were incredible. That day was pure joy.

But less than seventy-two hours earlier, my world was turned upside down with the single worst day of my life. Sitting at my desk, I think writing my sermon for the following Sunday, I received a call from my great-aunt telling me that my father was dead. His death was completely unexpected. He had just walked my sister down the aisle a couple of weeks earlier. My body went numb upon hearing the news, and then I let out a scream that caused my eight-and-a-half-month pregnant wife to come running to my office. My grandmother took the phone from her sister, and together we cried as she grieved the loss of her only living child and I the loss of my dad.

To say that my emotions were all over the place that first week of May 2005 would be the understatement of my life. I cried a lot, never sure if I was happy or sad. The pain of death and the glory of life were on full display for me and my family. One minute I was filled with a joy I had never known, completely delighted, and the next I was heartbroken, utterly devastated. It was, without question, the worst and best seventy-two hours of my life.

Ten years later, I remember that week like it was yesterday. There isn't a day gone by that I have not mourned my father nor given thanks for the life of my daughter as well as my wife, son, mother, and siblings. I still miss my dad a lot. From time to time, there are still tears and some very raw emotions.

But mine is not a unique experience. Most of us have seen death. We have been confronted with its pain up close and personal. This is the tragedy of our fallen, sinful world. Our bodies are not perfect. They will ultimately fail, and we will all die. A baptized child of God, he is among the communion of the saints, but my father was no saint. He was a wretched sinner, whose shortcomings I knew all too well. He loved the Lord and sought comfort in His Word and Sacraments, but my dad, like each of us, was never going to live forever.

All of us will die—some sooner than expected. But die we shall. This much is certain. And all of us will experience death, including those closest to us. We will feel its sting and cry out in pain. There are no simple words, no Hallmark cliché that can take the horror of death away. It is sure to come. And it sucks. It really, really sucks. For ten years, I have suffered its consequences, and I hate it today as much as I ever have.

Death however has no mastery over me. It may poke and prod and rear its ugly head. I will succumb to it one day, and those I love dearest will as well. But death will not win. As often as I experience it, as many times as I see and feel it, I will always find comfort in a joy that is far greater than death.

I say these things confidently, without any hesitation, because in this glorious Easter season, I know that my Redeemer lives. Christ is risen! He is risen from the dead. Death has no mastery over Him or to any who is part of His kingdom. On this birthday of my daughter and anniversary of my father's death, I am at peace. I am at peace in my Savior, who has forgiven me, as He has my father and my daughter. He has won eternal life for us, as He has for you. He has defeated death. He has conquered it—once for all—and in so doing, offers the joy of life with Him forever.

My father is dead, but one day he will rise with the Lord. My daughter is ten, and when this same Lord returns, she will be reunited with her grandfather. To God alone be the glory!

### William Rodney Rosenbladt, PhD
### (Dad Rod)
### Associate Professor of Theology and Apologetics
### Concordia University Irvine

## Frieda

As a young boy, I worked as a file clerk in my dad's medical office. I'd hear in the hallways some of the scuttlebutt. A beautiful, blonde, southern nurse (with whom I was sure I was in love) was sick, and my dad got wind of it. I happened to overhear the conversation in one of the examining rooms. "Frieda, are you sick today?" "Yes, Doctor." "Well, I want you to go home and get well, then." "My husband and I can't afford that, Doctor." "Frieda, I run this office, and you will be paid *anyway*. Now go home till you're well. And don't worry about the money. I'll make sure you are paid for those days."

## "I'd Work for Your Dad Anywhere!"

Once in a while, my dad's in-house lab tech, a Japanese gentleman, did what my dad (I think) suggested and introduced me to how to do simple lab analyses (CBCs, urinalyses, etc.) as part of my "work hours." During one of these sessions, Carl looked at me and asked, "Do you know why I work for your dad, Rod?" I answered, "No." Carl said, "Because he pays me *twice* what other lab techs are paid—*on the one condition that I never talk about it!* I'd work for your dad anytime and anywhere!"

## The Benefactor

I forget how I found out about it (certainly *not* from Dad!), but I learned from someone that every single semester, Dad would go to the University of Washington Medical School and ask which seniors were going to have to drop out for lack of money. Then he would pay for their whole last year's costs—*on the one condition that those students were never told where the money came from.*

## The MGA

Out of the blue, I got a phone call from my dad at my fraternity house. He asked, "Did you once say that you'd like a sports car?" I answered, "Dad, I'd love a sports car!" Dad said, "Well I just saved a young man's life in surgery, and he told me that he had bought an MGA convertible and that he *hates* the thing, wants to dump it ASAP. I think you need that MG, so I'm going to buy it." One of the first drives I took in it was up Hurricane Ridge (Olympic Rain Forest). It was night, and it wasn't long till I saw the flashing red lights behind me. The benevolent state trooper said to me, "You know, son, you weren't really breaking the speed laws. But when the signs say fifty miles per hour, you don't *have to take all the curves at fifty-five or sixty.*"

## Study Sessions

During my senior year of high school, a few friends and I would regularly plan to study together at my house in the evening. It would always last just a while, and we would end up playing poker instead. My dad would fix iced Coca-Colas and buttered popcorn, bring them down to us (we were "studying" in the basement), and noticed that we were playing poker. He would sit down for a few hands, lose $50, and then go upstairs again.

## Open Skies and Ammunition

My dad and his brother once bought an old farm overlooking the vast valley beneath it (came with the sale). It was in the old Ohop Valley, and the view to Mt. Rainier was both direct and relatively close. It had an old farmhouse (heated by a wood stove in the kitchen only) and an old crank phone where several parties "share with others." There were horses, cattle, pigs, and chickens so that my sister and I could watch things being born, learn to ride/care for horses, and learn to milk cows, and I could learn to drive on an old Ford tractor. In the closet of a first-floor bedroom, he stocked with ammunition of every imaginable caliber (.22; .38 Special; .45 Colt; shotgun shells, 12-gauge and .410; a hand trap and boxes of clay pigeons; rifles from .30-30 Winchester lever-action to Springfield Army, equivalent to what we today call .308). That was so that I could bring my schoolboy buddies up for a weekend and let them try shooting any rifle, handgun, or shotgun they wanted to. Dad would put them through a basic gun safety course and then turn them over to me to watch them carefully and enhance that training if necessary minute by minute. Their mothers were sure their sons were going to die that weekend, but the boys thought they had already died and gone to heaven. And the next time we came out to that farm, all the ammunition was seemingly magically *restocked*. It was like an ammunition cornucopia! The supply of ammunition never ran out.

## Hawaii

Once when I was in high school, dad came home from the office, looked around the dinner table, and said to all of us, "Go pack your bags. Tomorrow morning, we are flying to Hawaii for a couple of weeks."

## A Weekend in a Buick

A Buick salesperson was bugging Dad to trade in his Buick for a new one. Dad answered, "The one I've got now is just fine for the time being, but thanks." The guy would not stop: "Oh, Doc, just take this one for the weekend and try it." It was a '59 white convertible with red-and-white 'tuck-and-roll' upholstery. The guy wore dad down, and he consented. I had no idea of any of this but saw that beautiful convertible when I arrived at our Puget Sound beach place. Dad smiled, tossed me the keys to it, and said, "Have a good weekend!"

## Stealing Trees

On the drive to our Ohop Valley farm, we would pass by Ft. Lewis. One time, my dad pulled off to the side of the road and said "Come with me, Rod." He opened the car trunk, grabbed the tire iron and some newspaper, and started digging up some very small Douglas fir trees (he wanted to plant them on our beach property). He knew it was completely illegal (it was posted as such!). So we rushed to dig up about a dozen of those little trees, wrapped the roots in newspaper, and put them in the car trunk. All this was very, very hurried/rushed. In the rush of it all, we finished, and Dad quickly slammed the car trunk shut—and cut his favorite (and expensive) fly rod in half doing it! We got back in the car, and I realized it was a *perfect opportunity for a moral lecture on stealing from government property.*

Nope! Just hilarious laughter on his part, a laughter in which the whole family joined in.

### College Money

I was home from college (University of Washington) one weekend. During that time, my dad remarked, "How are you doing for money?" I replied, "I'm doing OK." Dad said, "No, you're not. It's not good to be poor—or close to it—while in college. I'll put some more in your account this week."

Davis Garton, MA
Concordia University Irvine

### Just Be There!

People who are into sports often speak about the abilities that athletes have that the average person doesn't have. He can run so fast! She can shoot the lights out! Wow, he can bench how much? But when it comes down to it, the most important ability any athlete can have is one that even the everyman can possess. Is the athlete available to play when needed? Is he there for his teammates when they need him most? The most important ability is availability.

My stepfather is as much the everyman as anyone I have ever met. He can't dunk a basketball. He isn't too talkative. He likes trains and watches the History Channel. He wears sweaters and goes to the fridge for a midnight snack every now and again. When I was growing up, he was the minivan-driving, crew cut–wearing, middle-managing everyman that we all know. And he was always there, always *available*.

If I had a little league baseball game, he was there watching quietly at the back of the stands. If I needed to be picked up from a friend's house at 7:00, he was there at 6:50 waiting, ready to drive me home when I was done. If my mom needed an ingredient at 9:00 p.m. for the dish she was making for her potluck the next day, he would be there for her, ready to drive to the store, fumble through the aisles, and come back with the right (or sometime wrong) item.

Some of my fondest memories as a young child were the times spent with the family after school. My brother and I played with our wooden blocks, building fort ramps to launch our other toys off. When my dad would come home from work, he would walk in the door and greet us, walk to his room, get changed, and then come back out, often without saying a word, and build forts with us. When we could smell the dinner that my mom was cooking, the three of us would wash our hands and sit down at the table, ready to eat as a family. At the table, before we could think about eating, he would pray for the meal and for our family—a simple, heartfelt prayer, but one he always said. He was a constant, loving presence in my life.

To this day, I can count on him to be there for my wife and me. He is available when our kitchen sink has a leak and we need him to bring over some tools. He is available if we need him to feed our cats when we are away for the weekend, even though he is allergic. Every Sunday he sits next to us at church, praising the Lord and listening to the message with us. He may not be the most interesting, the funniest, or the strongest man, but he is always there, ready to be my dad.

Gilbert Fugitt, EdD
Concordia University Irvine

### The Snow Drift

I remember one day in Kansas during a bad snowstorm that a man's truck went off the road into a snowdrift. His car stuck, he walked up to our house. We lived out in the country, and he needed a place to stay for the night, since the snowplow wasn't coming for a long time. I was told to give up my bed for the man. I realized after we had given him something to eat and he had taken a bath that truly everyone is your neighbor. The next day, when he was able to get going again, he simply said thank you. I learned from Dad that helping others isn't something we do because we might gain something from it; we are all in this world together, and we need to help each other.

### Daddy and Me

I now have two little girls of my own, and every Wednesday night, we go to Daddy and Me class. I have found that class isn't the important part . . . going to McDonald's before class is what they get excited about. They each get a Happy Meal, and I get an extra value meal;

however, the real "value" is that we have met Fernando, who is a custodian. He is a special needs person who knows the girls and has cleaned up their milk when they have spilled it. He always asks how they are doing. I try to emulate how my dad would take the time to talk with others. I don't want my girls to feel as if they are not allowed to know people who are different than them. When we rush around in this world, especially in Southern California, we forget that God has given us opportunities to impact people every day by just slowing down.

## Tullian Tchividjian, MDiv

### A Father's Love

When I was sixteen, my parents kicked me out of the house. They had tried everything. Nothing worked. And it got to the point where my lifestyle had become so disruptive to the rest of the household that they were left with no choice but to painfully say, "We love you, but you can't continue to live this way and live under our roof."

A couple years after they kicked me out, I was living in an apartment with a couple friends, and I called my dad (after losing yet another of my many dead-end jobs—I only called him when I needed something) and said, "Rent's due and I don't have any money." My dad asked, "Well, what happened to your job?" I made up some lie about cutbacks or something. He said, "Meet me at Denny's in an hour." I said OK. After we sat down, he signed a blank check, handed it to me, and said, "Take whatever you need. This should hold you over until you can find another job." He didn't probe into why I lost my job or yell at me for doing so. He didn't give a limit (here's $1,000). And I absolutely took advantage! I remember not only taking that check and writing it out for much more than I needed but also sneaking into my mom and dad's house on numerous occasions and stealing checks from out of his checkbook. I had mastered forging his signature. I went six months at one point without a job because I didn't need one! Any time I needed money, I would steal another check and forge his signature—$500, $300, $700. I completely took advantage of his kindness—and he knew it!

Years later he told me that he saw all those checks being cashed, but he decided not to say anything about it at the time. It didn't happen immediately (the fruits of grace are always in the future), but that demonstration of unconditional grace was the beginning of God doing a miraculous work in my heart and life. My dad's literal "turning of the other cheek" gave me a picture of God's unconditional love that I couldn't shake.

My father died in 2010, twenty-one years after he sent his disrespectful, ungrateful son on his way. And it was his unconditional, reckless, one-way love for me at my most arrogant and worst that God used to eventually bring me back. Until the day he died, my father was my biggest cheerleader and my best friend. I miss him every day.

Steve Brown once said, "Children will run from law and they'll run from grace. The ones who run from law rarely come back. But the ones who run from grace always come back. Grace draws its own back home." I ran from grace. It drew me home.

## Failure and One-Way Love

There wasn't one thing in particular that snapped me out of my "wild man" phase, no big crisis or single clarifying moment that inspired me to repair the damage I had done to myself, others, and my family. As humdrum as it may sound, what led me out of that rebellious period was simply the nagging sense that there had to be more to life than what I was experiencing—there had to be more to who I was than what this world was telling me. In fact, I can't even pinpoint the exact moment when God raised this dead rebel to life. All I know is that sometime in fall 1993, my culminating discontent with life made me decide to start going back to church.

I was twenty-one at the time. Kim, who had been my girlfriend for two years at that point, had actually started going to church with my parents a few months earlier, and before I knew it, we were both going every week. My parents were understandably overjoyed. Their prodigal had finally come home. "For this son of mine was dead and is alive again; he was lost and is found."[2]

Since Kim did not grow up in a Christian home like me, this was all brand new to her. But to me, it felt like a homecoming. Even in my unruly years, I had never really ceased to believe in God. In fact, if you had given me a theological exam at the height of my rebellion,

I would've passed with flying colors. I was just choosing to ignore it all. Maybe it was the timing, maybe it was the circumstances, but something finally clicked, and God became real to both of us in a new and exciting way.

About three months later, in January 1994, Kim and I got engaged. Our new faith naturally led us to take a hard look at our relationship. God was changing us, and we knew our relationship needed to change as well. After being so out of control for so long, we knew we had to adjust the way we related to each other, and the physical realm was no exception. We were both coming out of a world where sex outside of marriage was completely the norm—a norm that we had embraced—and we knew the right thing to do would be to pull back until we were married. Easier said than done!

Despite our best intentions and most earnest efforts, we slipped up three or four times during our engagement. I'll never forget when Kim came over to my apartment one night after work and told me she was pregnant. I was devastated. Not just because the news was a shock or because I hadn't expected to be a parent at such a young age; I was devastated because everyone who had celebrated my return "to the fold" would think the turnaround was a false alarm. I had caused my family so much pain and heartbreak with my self-absorbed shenanigans, and they had been so relieved and excited that their reckless son had finally come back; it had been the answer to years and years of prayer. I had put my parents through more than any son ever should and had asked for their forgiveness on numerous occasions. To drop this bomb might crush them all over again, and I just couldn't bear it. I was scared, ashamed, and angry at myself for failing yet again.

Somehow we summoned the courage to go over to my mom and dad's house the next day—Mother's Day, believe it or not. After some awkward small talk, I asked my father if we could speak to him alone. We walked out to the driveway. Dad was standing in front of me, and Kim was by my side, shoulder to shoulder. "Dad, we have something to tell you." I burst into tears. "Kim's pregnant." Kim started bawling too. Next thing I knew, he was embracing both of us, me with one arm, her with the other, while we wept. He held us for ten minutes. He could see how overwhelmed we were. I can still hear his voice telling us, "It's OK. We love you. It's going to be OK. This child is going to be a blessing."

Kim and I had been so excited about getting married, and now we were going to be parents as well. In addition to the embarrassment and shame involved, we were grieving the happy expectation that we'd have a few years, just the two of us, before starting a family. We were in a state of shock. Yet my father did not condemn or lecture us, even though he had every right to do so. Instead, he comforted us. More than that, he gave us good news. He told us that while the circumstances clearly weren't ideal, this was going to turn out just fine. This baby was going to be a blessing to both of us and a gift to the whole family. Every time Kim and I look at our oldest son (now eighteen), we realize afresh that my dad was absolutely right that day.

The whole situation was wrapped in grace: I deserved his reproach and disapproval—premarital sex resulting in unexpected pregnancy is no father's dream for his child—yet his gracious response assured me that he not only wasn't crushed, his love for me was stronger than ever. When I told him (through many tears) how sorry I was for once again letting him down, he simply hushed me by hugging me tighter and saying over and over again, "It's OK. I love you. It's OK. I love you." At that moment in the driveway, when I rightly deserved my dad's disappointment, he assured me of his delight. Even now it is hard to put into words the emotional relief I felt. Lifesaving is not too strong a word. I thank God with every fiber of my being that He put me in a family where I was surrounded by such one-way love.

The love my father showed me that day is not a one-to-one approximation of God's one-way love for you and me—nothing is! But this act of grace served as an accurate reflection of that one true Act of Grace, or one-way love, to which all others point. That is, he treated me in a way that was analogous to how God treats you and me. He was not God, of course, but like many fathers, he did play a similar role in my life: someone in authority who showed me love in the midst of deserved judgment. And like that One True Act of Grace, my father's forgiveness and love changed me forever.

# CHAPTER 10

# The Father in Everyday Life

The idea of the father as an analogy of being (*analogia entis*) to a gracious God offers a theological way of thinking about fatherhood. This analogy of being provides a theological way to think about how the father and fatherhood generally influence the family as well. Recovering a theology of fatherhood, or an apologetic from fatherhood, can help men influence their family on a deeper level as they attempt to carry their faith to their vocation as father.

This apologetic is more than just a defense of the faith; it is a theology of how to live as a father. It has to do not only with how our children are brought to the faith but with our own sanctification and good works as fathers. In this way, it is a theology of the day-to-day life of the dad in the home. What it tells us is that it is not necessary for Christian fathers to be "specifically called" to the Church in order to be evangelists and apologists for the Christian faith, nor is fatherhood to be seen as some complicated set of theological propositions. Rather, fatherhood is lived, and children are evangelized vocationally. It is in the ostensibly ordinary experiences that a father provides the magic as well as how the evangelistic and apologetic work occurs. Fatherhood is thus to be lived out in the family, whatever that makeup looks like in its various incarnations. This may seem somewhat mundane, but it is our own sin that makes it seem that way. To God and to our children, it is in the magic of the Gospel. Living out life as a gracious dad in a family is one way in which we become a "little Christ" to the world.

## The Father and His Two Lost and Found Sons

This work relied on the parable of the prodigal son in order to build a model concerning the father's evangelistic and apologetic role in the home. From it, we gain a picture of who God the Father is and how He is seen by way of analogy through the actions of an earthly father. The story of the two sons is our story. One son is outwardly rebellious and the other sanctimonious and self-righteous. Both sons are in need of forgiveness and neither trusting in the grace of the father to provide it. Yet in both cases, the father's love is evident in his willingness to forgive:

> But while he was still a long way off, his father saw him and felt compassion, and ran and embraced him and kissed him. And the son said to him, 'Father, I have sinned against heaven and before you. I am no longer worthy to be called your son.' But the father said to his servants, 'Bring quickly the best robe, and put it on him, and put a ring on his hand, and shoes on his feet. And bring the fattened calf and kill it, and let us eat and celebrate. For this my son was dead, and is alive again; he was lost, and is found.' And they began to celebrate.[1]

The father, in this our paramount example of fatherhood, is called to be a forgiver. This is his personal task. As fathers, this too is our personal task, our calling, our vocation—as forgivers.

I have argued in this book that the vocation of father is worked out in many different arenas that serve as the stage for our various other vocations: masculine man, husband, dad, bringer of magic, provider, and head of the home. Each of these is crucial to the task. Together, they constitute what it means to be a father. When God first established the vocation of father, it seems he had in mind that it would be acted out by means of the day-to-day parts of our being as men called to be fruitful and multiply. And yet one thing was left out of this description. Christian fathers, who are called to be good dads, are first called to the faith—that is, called to be Christians.

In the Psalms, we read, "As a father has compassion on his children, so the LORD has compassion on those who fear him."[2] It seems that having compassion is part and parcel with being a father. Compassion and forgiveness are personal characteristics that fathers are blessed with according to the natural order of things as intended by

God. So of course, then, not all fathers are compassionate. But for a father to lack compassion seems to be an aberration and not the norm. Thus fathers, according to the natural order of things, delight in their children: "Sons are a heritage from the LORD, children a reward from him. Like arrows in the hands of a warrior are sons born in one's youth. Blessed is the man whose quiver is full of them. They will not be put to shame when they contend with their enemies in the gate."[3]

As we examined earlier, children are called to love and honor their parents, and this has a promise: "Honor your father and your mother, that your days may be long in the land that the Lord your God is giving you."[4] Yet fathers have a call and command too. A father's job is to instruct; it is his job to not exasperate his children but bring them up in the mercy of the Lord: "Children, obey your parents in the Lord, for this is right. 'Honor your father and mother,' which is the first commandment with a promise— 'that it may go well with you and that you may enjoy long life on the earth.' Fathers, do not exasperate your children; instead, bring them up in the training and instruction of the Lord."[5]

## Live as the Men You Are Called to Be

Living as the men we have been called to be means that we live as men who love. The Apostle Paul is clear about this in 1 Corinthians when he claims that no matter what we say, if we speak without love, we are no better than a banging gong:

> If I speak in the tongues of men and of angels, but have not love, I am only a resounding gong or a clanging cymbal. If I have the gift of prophecy and can fathom all mysteries and all knowledge, and if I have a faith that can move mountains, but have not love, I am nothing. If I give all I possess to the poor and surrender my body to the flames, but have not love, I gain nothing. Love is patient, love is kind. It does not envy, it does not boast, it is not proud. It is not rude, it is not self-seeking, it is not easily angered, it keeps no record of wrongs. Love does not delight in evil but rejoices with the truth. It always protects, always trusts, always hopes, always perseveres. Love never fails. But where there are prophecies, they will cease; where there are tongues, they will be stilled; where there is knowledge, it will pass

away. For we know in part and we prophesy in part, but when perfection comes, the imperfect disappears. When I was a child, I talked like a child, I thought like a child, I reasoned like a child. When I became a man, I put childish ways behind me. Now we see but a poor reflection as in a mirror; then we shall see face to face. Now I know in part; then I shall know fully, even as I am fully known. And now these three remain: faith, hope and love. But the greatest of these is love.[6]

So in one sense, it does not matter how your father treated you. It maybe does not even matter if you had a father. What matters is who you are. You are a free child of God, and if you are reading this, you are probably a father. Those who have been called to faith have also been called to freedom in Christ. It is that freedom that allows us to truly love. Paul can say what he does in 1 Corinthians 13 because he is not talking to those who are yet slaves to the Law and the death it brings. Christ is the end of the Law for us.[7] We are free. Being free, we are now free to be servants to one another in love. That is why love is the greatest, because its origin is freedom. So in turn, we too are free to forgive.

Some will criticize the idea that the father has a particular order in life, in the family, and in the home because what is presented here may seem like some kind of backward antiquated social order. Yet we know from God's Word that He more often than not tends to work through these social orders how and why He chooses to do so.[8] Vocationally, the role of the father will always be different than that of mother. We may choose to deny this reality, but our denial does not equate to changing the way things are.

The best way to understand this is again to visit the paramount analogy to God as our Father that we have in the text. The parable of the prodigal son is the channel through which we come to an understanding of grace, forgiveness, and a father's compassion on his children. The father's vocation in the tale is made up of all the ancillary vocations spoken of earlier: masculine man, husband, dad, bringer of magic, provider, and head of the home. This is not a static order. Rather, this presentation is active and alive and is even interactive in the way it plays out. The father is not permissive of any wrongdoing; rather, he promotes freedom and gives forgiveness.

The whole of Scripture speaks against a denial of this order. The father is to speak in encouragement and love to exhort his family in the love of the Lord: "For you know how, like a father with his children, we exhorted each one of you and encouraged you and charged you to walk in a manner worthy of God, who calls you into his own kingdom and glory."[9] Further, he is the head of the house: "For the husband is the head of the wife even as Christ is the head of the church, his body, and is himself its Savior."[10] But his headship is intended to point to love, forgiveness, and encouragement. It is not a headship that lords power over those whom he is called to serve. It is a headship meant to be that *analogia entis* to a good and gracious God.

In *God at Work*, Gene Veith describes the reality that as Christians, we do not give up the natural order of things or our earthly vocations, but rather we now embrace them in freedom and love. Veith explains that "when He says to live as you were called, he is saying, among other things, do not change your various vocations just because you became a Christian."[11] Rather, understand that God's order, or first use of the Law, is still in place among Christians.

Thus we acknowledge that some things we do as men, rightly and wrongly, support our vocations as father, while others detract from it. When we use our power to serve only as a means of punishment and intimidation, we detract from our intended headship and fatherhood. When we disrespect our calling as husband to our wife, we teach our children that our grace has limits. When we fail to love, we show that we misunderstand what it takes for God to love us—namely, the atonement wrought by His own Son. But the Gospel changes all that. The Gospel breaks in and speaks peace, hope, deliverance, forgiveness, and love into our hearts. And on that powerful Word of life, we ride into the lives of our families speaking those same words of peace, hope, deliverance, forgiveness, and love. When we do this, our headship in the family is confirmed. When we do this, we teach our children that God's grace has no limits because it took a limitless grace to forgive us. When we act in love, we merely shadow God's love as a pale reflection. But sometimes that pale reflection is just what is needed to provide hope!

The real-life application seems to be that as fathers, we need to accept our vocations as handed down to us, or gifted to us, by God. This means being confident in our state of being as fathers; not desiring to be something we are not, but recognizing our fatherhood as a gift from God. It also means that there is no need for us to deny our other various vocations for the sake of fatherhood. A masculine man can be a good father and ought to be. But more often than not, that strength will be shown in love. A father ought to be first a husband, and he too should recognize that to be his first calling in the home. If a father and mother approach the life of the family together, only then will a father be free to be a "good dad."

Even bad fathers can learn to be good dads. The Christian life is full of ups and downs. People mature and learn to grow in the faith. If you are reading this book, I suspect it is because you are a good father in need of encouragement or a struggling father in need of help. As I have said from the beginning, this book is not necessarily intended to be a how-to manual of fathering. It may certainly be that at times, but it is intended to encourage you with love. My intent is to show you the importance of your vocation as a dad. This is a calling so great that it literally points your children in a real and substantial way to the cross of Christ and a gracious God who loves them and desires them as His children. My only words of intentionally practical advice to you will be this: You are forgiven in Christ. He has called you to Himself and to be a dad. Be confident in God's purpose for you as a father. As a father, you are in a position to be an analogy of being to a good God. God has called you to this and you are merely walking in the steps that He has laid out for you. Live freely as the dad God has called you to be.

## A Father's Rest

As Dad Rod said, "When good fathers die, it is always too soon." As I began the story of my own fatherhood, I confessed that I never knew my father. Though I never knew him, I miss him every day. I long to hear his voice today as much as I believe I did the day I was born. He is a part of me, and my *analogia entis* sometimes works in reverse. I know that my God loves me and is my Father. When I read the prodigal son, I know it is my Father in Heaven that is being described, but I can't help but substitute my own mental image of my dad. All our dads will come to blessed rest one day, and we will be left here to await our reunion in paradise. George Macdonald echoes the deep ache of our father's loss.

To My Father

Take of the first fruits, Father, of thy care,
Wrapped in the fresh leaves of my gratitude
Late waked for early gifts ill understood;
Claiming in all my harvests rightful share,
Whether with song that mounts the joyful air
I praise my God; or, in yet deeper mood,
Sit dumb because I know a speechless good,
Needing no voice, but all the soul for prayer.
Thou hast been faithful to my highest need;
And I, thy debtor, ever, evermore,
Shall never feel the grateful burden sore.
Yet most I thank thee, not for any deed,
But for the sense thy living self did breed
That fatherhood is at the great world's core.


All childhood, reverence clothed thee, undefined,
As for some being of another race;
Ah! not with it departing—grown apace
As years have brought me manhood's loftier mind
Able to see thy human life behind—
The same hid heart, the same revealing face—
My own dim contest settling into grace
Of sorrow, strife, and victory combined.
So I beheld my God, in childhood's morn,
A mist, a darkness, great, and far apart,
Moveless and dim—I scarce could say Thou art:
My manhood came, of joy and sadness born—
Full soon the misty dark, asunder torn,
Revealed man's glory, God's great human heart.[12]

George MacDonald
Algiers, April, 1857.


We, too, as fathers will face our last summons, and we will die. We will leave our sons and daughters here and will go to be with our Heavenly Father. At that point, we will no longer rely solely on the pale reflection that is all things of this earth. Rather we will see Him face to face. At that point, having been called home in the Faith, we will hear our Father say, "Well done, good and faithful servant. You have been faithful over a little; I will set you over much. Enter into the joy of your master."[13] Further, the text tells us that our response will be, "We are unworthy servants; we have only done what was our duty."[14] Every father has answered the question "Dad, I am your son, right?" or "Daddy, I am your little girl, right?" When we are face to face with the Lord and claim that we are but His dutiful servants, we are simply acknowledging that He knows who we are. It is no more a puffed up resonation than the voice of a child asking his or her father to acknowledge him or her as his.

You are a father. You are someone's precious daddy. You will, at times, ask yourself, What good am I doing? The days spent cleaning up messes and fixing broken things will at times overwhelm you. But you too are an *analogia entis* to the good and gracious Father who desires to forgive. He shadows that forgiveness in you. He also desires to give you that forgiveness when you fail. Be confident in your office, in your vocation as dad. Know that your children long for your voice as you long for the Father's voice to tell you, "Well done, good and faithful servant. You have been faithful over a little; I will set you over much. Enter into the joy of your master." Be their little Christ, and you will give them the gift of knowing first hand that it will all work out to His good end. As our Lord told us, "My Father, who has given them to me, is greater than all, and no one is able to snatch them out of the Father's hand."[15] It is all in the Father's hands.

The End

# Epilogues

## Why Daughters Need Fathers

*Joyce L. C. Keith*

For Scott and me, one of our happiest days together was the day before Reformation Day 1999. Just after midnight, I gave birth to our last child, a seven-pound two-ounce, twenty-inch baby girl with red hair and bright blue eyes. We named her Autumn Whitney Grace. She was thrown into her father's arms, who had not only tears of joy in his eyes but now shaking knees and a panicked heart, as the doctor swept me off to emergency surgery. At that moment, he was holding our third child and praying without ceasing that he wouldn't have to go it alone. He was scared to say the least, but there he was holding this precious little girl. A little girl! When we had found out that we were having a baby girl, he looked me straight in the eye and said, "Keiths don't make girls!" Well, I had the ultrasound picture to prove otherwise, and as the next three months went by quickly up in the mountains of Lake Arrowhead, California, we purchased pink things and debated over what to name this girl that was coming soon. Fifteen years later, he looks at her with the same joy that he did that day in 1999. He is not so panicked anymore. He just loves her. It is a love that unfortunately I did not have with my father, except on a few occasions.

My earliest memories are of my dad giving me horsey rides in the living room of our brick bungalow house in Chicago. My dad was a very large man. He was a giant as far as I was concerned, standing at six feet three inches with big, bright, blue eyes and black hair. For as long as I can remember, he always struggled with his weight.

Sometimes he was as thin as 220 pounds, and a couple of times I remember he was tipping the scales around 400 pounds. Nonetheless, he was always a big guy. When we would be driving home late at night coming from a party of some kind, I used to pretend faking being asleep. I wanted those big, strong arms to carry me up the front stairs and into the house, take off my shoes, and tuck me safe and warm into bed. That was my dad when I was a little girl. Girls love those giant men. Dads are "giants," you know? I was maybe two or three feet tall; to us, you look as if you can touch the clouds. You can reach everything. Our dad is our knight in shining armor. You can slay dragons and rescue the princess from her imminent danger. You can throw me up into the air, and I'll never fear falling. I'll express screams of glee. I'll cling onto your leg and have you walk around the house with me because you're so strong. You are my dad!

I was very sick for most of my kindergarten year, in and out of hospitals, and I remember him coming in very early in the morning. I would wake up with the sun just breaking through and see the shadow of that giant, heartbroken man sitting and weeping next to my bed. He would have just gotten home from the night shift and would sit beside me before he headed off to bed. He would hold my frail hand and tell me he loved me, and then he would kiss my fevered forehead and head to the hall, trying to hide his tears as he swiftly left the room. I could see his shoulders shaking as he tried to keep his fear from me. Dads *love* their daughters.

Unfortunately, our daughter was also very sick in her kindergarten year. She had a horrible, mysterious, itchy rash that covered most of her body, and it moved! She was stricken with a severe fever, and the doctors were baffled for months. Her father would so tenderly pour Epsom salt bath water over her shivering body in an attempt to bring down her fevers. She was the queen of the tea party baths, and hot water was not allowed, so dad found a way to make it work. She was tough; she hardly ever scratched and became a voracious reader that year. She still is to this day. But as she got better, her dad was the first one to make sure she continued to learn how to do all the things her big brothers were doing: skateboarding, cycling, swimming, running. She would do everything they did, and her dad would make sure that if she wanted to do something, we would get her whatever she needed to do it. He was giving her bits of magic. A custom-built skateboard, the coolest bike whenever she outgrew the last one, goggles to fit her teeny-tiny little head, horseback riding lessons—he gave her all these things to let her know that her needs would always be met and met with immediate fulfillment. You could say she was spoiled, but you could also say that her dad loved her very much.

But what happens? Why do so many dads stop showing that love? Why, oh why, when we start to find a little attitude and self-expression, do you let us walk away? In chapter 7, my husband addresses a possible reason. He talks about how when a man's job is taken away, he is likely to let it go. Men, as I've come to find, are simple. Yes, you like sports, your favorite shirt that you've had since college, and your movies or whatever; you are simple. We girls sometimes learn this and bat our eyelashes and call you "daddy" to get you to give us what we want. We know how to ask for what we want. But when we tell you—or sometimes we don't tell you—that we don't want you to talk to us about a certain subject (boys, our hair, the new makeup that we put on, or the fact that we're getting to be a young lady and will have periods and wear bras), it doesn't mean that you should stop spending time with us. We are still and always will be your daughters. We may not be three feet tall anymore, but your arms are always a strong refuge.

## Your Daughter's Voice

Your wife is not your daughter's voice. If you want your relationship with your daughter to continue, you need to talk to her. You are not her BFF either. You are her dad. You changed her diapers, and you walked her when she was fussy and cried for what seemed to be hours. You drove her around the block until she fell asleep. Why stop doing what's necessary? You are allowed to tell us that the clothes we may have chosen aren't OK. One of the best stories I've heard on this subject is from our friend Jill. When Jill was in junior high one day, she decided to dress as all the other girls were dressing, but this wasn't what she normally wore. You know, the cool kids were all doing it! Her skirt was obviously too short and her shirt was not becoming, and her dad looked her straight in the eye, took her by the hand, and said, "Jill, you are so much prettier than those clothes." That was it. He didn't insult her, he didn't raise his voice, and he surely didn't punish her. He just let her know that she was his beautiful daughter. He was aware of who she was, and he told her that she was pretty. End of story! She says that she never put on another provocative piece of clothing. Why would she ever let clothing that gave away her dignity and even took away from her beauty be put on her body? Her dad loved her, and he told her so. And she respected his words without argument.

## My Magic with My Dad

My dad and I had a special couple of times a year when we would go clothes shopping. I can remember from when I was three or four going to boutiques with my dad. Every time we would go shopping, he bought me an outfit of my choice. I would grab armfuls of things to try on in the dressing room. He would find a chair outside and tell me what he thought of each and every outfit. We shopped for hours. Then he would tell me to pick one, or sometimes—after he must have earned a special bonus at work—he would tell me to get them all! Magic!!! My dad was the guy who took me shopping for my prom dress. I even insisted that he come with me to shop for my wedding dress. Each time I needed to come home on the weekends from college, my dad was the guy who would pick me up and ask if I needed a new pair of jeans. We would stop at the mall on the way home. My mom would see the bags and would just roll her eyes. He would come for a visit to see the grand babies and would always take me out for a day of shopping. Magic!

Sadly, my dad is gone now. He suffered terribly in his last few years with depression and eventually took his own life one Saturday morning in spring 2012. My heart aches to hear his voice. I miss him so much, and I could never imagine that it would still be this hard so many years later. He wasn't the best dad, but he was my dad. He let go of me too soon when I was becoming a young lady, but his eyes were never happier than the day he gave me away to my husband. Again, in his giant form, he walked with me arm in arm down the aisle, slightly shaking as he, with pinkies out, lifted my veil, kissed me, and handed me to Scott. He tried to hold back the tears, but again his shoulders gave him away. We danced our father-daughter dance together as two people who had such a strong tie that bound us from my birth.

Daughters need their dads. I didn't see my dad very often in his last few years, as we lived many miles apart. He would spend most days locked in his dark bedroom. My mom could hardly get him to come out, but when I did make it to their home, I would go in to see that giant man in his frail state, and I would take him by the hand, kiss his forehead, and tell him that I loved him and that dinner was at five. I was cooking, and right at five, I'd see him at the table. He'd eat, smile, and start to become my dad again, because dads don't like to look weak to their daughters even in their worst state.

He called me about a week before he died. You know how you never forget the last time you talked to someone? I was sitting in my car at an airport, waiting to pick up Scott when my dad called me. He talked to me in one of the happiest tones I heard him speak in years. We had a great conversation. It was nothing short of a miracle. My dad sounded strong and more like himself, more like the way I had always remembered. I know he wanted to hide how he was really feeling. He never wanted his daughter to see him that way. Days later, my mom called.

I still need my dad. I will see him again in heaven. As Jim Nestingen reminded me as we drove down to be with my mom that same day, "Blessed are the poor in spirit, for they will see God." I will always see my dad as strong. He was brave, tall, and enormous, and he will always be that to me. He was the first glimpse of what I wanted to find in my own husband. He treated my mom like a queen. I saw with my own eyes what a long-lasting, committed marriage was supposed to look like, both good days and bad days. They had been married just a week shy of forty-five years! My mom never left him, which I hear is nothing short of a miracle itself. He taught me how to shoot a gun, clean a fish, and be a well-mannered, respectable young lady who grew to be the best wife and mom he could have wished for me to be. Those strong hands will always be what I think of when I think of my father. They carried me to bed even when he knew I was faking sleep; he didn't mind. Dads never really mind being a bit of magic for their daughters, do they? Just don't ever let it stop because, even as we all age, we still have a special connection as father and daughter. We will always need you.

# Why Sons Need Fathers

## *Dr. Rod Rosenbladt*

I remember that Paul Fairweather would comment that women, and especially mothers, are experts on the body and our bodily needs. If that is true, it makes sense then that women will always know about ninety times more about the physical needs of children than any man does.

Fathers, on the other hand, are the source of "inspiration" to their children, though not in the biblical or "Delphic oracle" sense. I think what Paul was getting at is close to what we all talk about when we talk of "aspiring." Absent a father, sons don't "aspire," or even know how to "aspire"; it is at the least fleeting and at the most absent in their consciousness.

Paul would also teach us that any and all fathers who just "are fathers" are, in one way or another—more being than doing—telling their sons that the Law is not, will not be, the "final" voice in the universe.

Daily, sons are given this—not as "lectures" but just by their fathers watching them, listening to them, being with them. Most men would worry here about "chaos," "anarchy," "shirking the teaching of responsibility," and so on. Paul did not. He was operating at the level of "what the child/son needs" more than worrying about the ten ways things can go south. The rationale for him came not from formal training but rather from the way his own father related to him from the earliest days.

Once Paul's son was called in by the school for "being irresponsible." To make things more serious, they asked his dad to be there for that. Paul turned the tables on the school and said to the principal that evidently the school provided next to nothing worth his son "responding to"! Paul rescued his son that day. That is what dads do.

Paul would often imply that sons desperately needed fathers because it is impossible for sons to "invent" a father. It just can't be done. And when the fatherless sons attempt it, it always comes out as a category of "power" and becomes the fuel for urban gang building and recruiting. It's what it looks like to them in their bereft imaginations. And, of course, it's not (finally) their fault. What they really needed was a dad—every single day. Such boys would have daily seen that their fathers, finally, aren't defined by power; they are defined by grace (as you've so often heard me say). Fathers are living, breathing analogies—who say, just by their quiet being, that there is something (Someone?) in the universe who will override the Law and will not allow the Law to be "the last word."

Will fathers be involved in some discipline stuff? Yes, of course. But again, Paul would say that we fathers are not really "wired" for that. We do it—particularly when the situation is in some way "dire"—but we do not umpire each and every little thing the way a mom often has to do all day, every day. Mom recognizes that she is better equipped for adjudicating family righteousness and some-times will actually say that it is her *vocatio* in a way that it isn't the same as for the kids' dad. It is rare, but it is like a gift from heaven itself if she "gets" that and will say it!

You've probably heard me quote Paul: "The calling of being a mother isn't just hard. It's impossible!" It was hyperbole, but he was (like Luther?) using hyperbole, I think, to get a point across to all us men: "Don't ever take what a good mom does every day with your kids for granted, guys! Ever!"

It makes me think of the movie *Mr. Mom.* The premise of the woman working and the man at home with kids is portrayed so well: he is overwhelmed, out of his element, doing something foreign to him every single hour, at his wit's end, and laughingly inept. But if a moviemaker can portray such a difference and hold it up for everyone to look at, there must be something that is "universal" or "common" about it. If not, why do we laugh and cry? It's recognition somehow that "there is a real difference"—and not because of "social conditioning," either. It's ontic.

Every single hour, every single instance of Mom or Dad—especially up to age seven—goes into a child and forms him or her. Think of experiments with, say, ducklings and "imprinting." There is a window of time when even animals get who their mothers are. Substitute a mechanical mom sometime during that window, and the young will from then on see the mechanical mom as the real one. I think most psychologists say that once it is imprinted, it's forever and can't be later erased by the real mom duck no matter what. Paul used to ask us all, "What does a child miss?" And his answer was, "Nothing!" It all goes in, no filtering. And it all is always "forming" a son or daughter, meeting their real needs or not.

The "upside" to this is what Paul was wont to say: "Health is relatively simple, straightforward. It's neurosis that is labyrinthine, complicated, like a maze."

He once said to me, "You owe a very great debt, Rod, to some-one you've never heard of or met." Of course, I asked why. He said, "From your description of your paternal grandfather and your pater-nal grandmother, I know that some older man deeply helped your dad to define [inadequate word] who he was. A man like your dad could not have been what he obviously was, given only your grand-parents. Some older man really, really helped him along the way."

Many of the wonderful gifts my father gave me from my earli-est years became conscious to me only much, much later. I suppose that's not all that unusual in the case of fathers and sons.

Some are so basic that they are all too easy to take for granted. I think of growing up as a boy in a house that my father made sure was safe. Here I'm not thinking so much of from dangerous crimi-nals as I am from awful arbitrariness. I later learned that children who grow up in relatively lousy homes could even survive that. The thing that devastates a young son or daughter is an environment in which the rules are always changing and never to be counted on day by day. That's the killer. I could "bet the farm" each and every day on my father's stable, gracious character. It didn't vary. And though he hardly reared us, he "over the long haul" demonstrated that a father can be the same day after day, month after month. Fathers need not be different people depending on the ever-changing circumstances of daily life. I had no idea how common it was for children to very quickly "get a read" on Dad's mood when he came home from work. I didn't have to do that. And I took that for granted as a young boy and never realized what a great gift it was.

Another thing I—again, only later—appreciated about my dad was that he was conscious of my needs as a boy, even when I was clueless. I needed to learn early on what it was to work but didn't know that. My dad offered to make me a lowly file clerk in his med-ical office. It was not all that impressive, even as I write this. But he knew that it was important for a son to learn how to get up, dress up, and show up to work. And it is important. He did not just growl at me, "You should go find yourself a job somewhere, Rod." He provided one based on the real needs in his office. That way, I could learn the nature of having a job with him as my boss! Again, this is fairly basic. But consider how many American boys today do not have that opportunity, how many boys grow up having missed learning what having a job is during those key early years. They are on our streets, believing that someone—the government—should be sending them a check for no reason whatsoever.

Another aspect that was a gift from my dad was the complete absence of what psychologists call "generational confusion." I think of the number of daughters who were taught early on that their calling in life was to "mother their own mothers." It is a ghastly confusion perpetrated against you women. A woman psychotherapist friend once called it "trying to be your own grandmother!" Blessedly, it was completely absent in my dad. I was never told, even implicitly, that part of being a son was to take care of my dad. From him it was clearly and always, "My calling is to take care of *you*—not the other way around." Looking back, I think my dad realized that his life might turn out to be shorter than the lives of other men (he had rheumatic fever as a boy, and that does lasting damage to the heart). And my bet is that, in his mind, it became something like, "If my life is going to be short, I've got to 'make count' each and every day—for my son and for my daughter!" Sure enough, my dad was forced to go to the Mayo Clinic for diagnostic work when he was only fifty-two (tricuspid dorsal aortic valve). In 1962, it had just become possible to replace that valve. But in those early days, there was no MRI. The surgeon just went in, found out the extent of the damage, measured, and then ordered a new valve in another room. It was then brought to the operating room to be installed. And what did the surgeon discover in my dad's chest once he was in? It was the heart of an eighty-year-old in the chest of a fifty-two-year-old man! Two of the three valves had been calcified for years, and his heart had pumped through just one-third of the opening it should have had. Dad never got off the heart-lung machine. He died on the table. I tell this story because I think my dad had, for years, packed me and my sister's childhoods, based on the assumption that he would not have as many years to father us as other men had. It turned out he was right.

Many have heard stories from me already about my dad that illustrate his amazing grace (e.g., me drunk, stacking up my old Buick). But that wasn't anywhere near unusual in my dad's case. Pastors know of this amazing grace, having to exposit the nature of mercy in the biblical writings. And especially in Jesus's parables, it is nothing short of amazing given our state after the Fall. (As I've said in other contexts, put mercy into the hands of a great filmmaker and it will jar every viewer!) But beyond God's mercy in the Bible is God's grace. Perhaps the greatest example of this is the parable of what turns out to be "The Two Prodigal Sons" in Luke 15. Read the explication of the late Father Robert Capon or read almost any book by Pastor Tullian Tchividjian. I won't retell my stories (there are many of them), but my point here is that from my dad, I learned "grace" again and again. Not by what he said, but by what he was and what he did. Over and over, in many and manifest ways, I learned from my dad what God's grace is. And every instance of it is still emblazoned in my memory. How he managed to do that with a son like me is still—every day—amazing to me. I was constantly being not just forgiven but regiven the full inheritance! Mercy can be, "All right. I'll cancel your debt and you can 'start over.'" But grace is even more. It is more than "starting over." Grace is the regranting of full inheritance after a colossal screw-up! It is even greater than mercy! Dad was doing what our Lutheran Confessions call the *favor dei propter Christum* (the favor of God on account of Christ) with me—not just once but time after time.

# Notes

## Chapter 1

1 See Paul Fairweather, *Father Presence: The Obscure Voice of Empathy* (Aliso Viejo, CA: Author, 1997).

2 "Facts for Features: Unmarried and Single Americans Week: September 19–25, 2010," U.S. Census Bureau, accessed May 25, 2015, https://www.census.gov/newsroom/releases/archives/facts_for_features_special_editions/cb10-ff18.html.

3 Michael S. Oden, *When Nobody's Home: The Truth behind Drug and Alcohol Addiction through the Eyes of a Probation Officer* (Bloomington, IN: Author House, 2014), 15–16.

4 Ibid.

5 *Criminal Justice and Behavior* 14 (1978): 403–26.

6 David Popenoe, *Life without Father: Compelling New Evidence That Fatherhood and Marriage Are Indispensable for the Good of Children and Society* (New York: Free Press, 1996), 152. Popenoe notes that the dropout rates for children born out of wedlock are 37 percent and 31 percent for children in divorced households compared with only 13 percent for nondisrupted families. Popenoe's data originated from a study conducted by Sara McLanahan and Gary Sandefur. See also, Sara McLanahan and Gary D. Sandefur, *Growing Up with a Single Parent: What Hurts, What Helps* (Cambridge, MA: Harvard University Press, 1994), 67–68.

7 Robbie Low, "The Truth about Men and Church," *Touchstone: A Journal of Mere Christianity* 16, no. 5 (2003); see also Werner Haug et al., "The Demographic Characteristics of National Minorities in Certain European States," Council of Europe Directorate General III, Social Cohesion, no. 31 (Strasbourg: 2000).

8 Ibid.

9 2 Corinthians 15:19.

10 Romans 5:8.

11 Romans 1:16.

12 James Arne Nestingen and Gerhard O. Forde, *Free to Be: A Handbook to Luther's Small Catechism* (Minneapolis, MN: Augsburg, 1975), 201–6.

13 Helmut Thielicke, *The Waiting Father; Sermons on the Parables of Jesus* (New York: Harper, 1959), 12.

14 Gustaf Wingren, *The Living Word: A Theological Study of Preaching and the Church* (Philadelphia: Muhlenberg, 1960), 140.

15 Martin Luther, *Commentary on the Epistle to the Galatians* (Grand Rapids, MI: Zondervan, 1949), 5.

# Chapter 2

1 Fairweather, *Father Presence*, 1–10.

2 Luke 15:11–32.

3 Robert Farrar Capon, *The Parables of Grace* (Grand Rapids, MI: Wm. B. Eerdmans, 1988), 138–40.

4 Romans 3:24.

5 Capon, *Parables of Grace*, 140.

6 Luke 15:21.

7 Luke 15:22.

8 Isaiah 61:10.

9 Luke 15:29.

10 Luke 15:30.

11 Capon, *Parables of Grace*, 144.

12 Ibid.

13 Capon, *Parables of Grace*, 141.

14 John 14:6.

15 John 10:30.

16 Romans 5:19.

# Chapter 3

1 C. S. Lewis, *The Four Loves* (New York: Harcourt, Brace, 1960), 57–61.

2 Robert Bly, *Iron John: A Book about Men* (Cambridge, MA: Da Capo, 2004), 61.

3 Ibid., 62.

4 Laughlin, "Who's Minding the Kids? Child Care Arrangements: Spring 2011," U.S. Census Bureau, accessed May 28, 2015, https://www.census.gov/prod/2013pubs/p70-135.pdf.

# Chapter 4

1 Ephesians 5:25.

2 Genesis 2:23.

3 Adapted from Gene Edward Veith, *God at Work: Your Christian Vocation in All Life* (Wheaton, IL: Crossway Books, 2002), 77–78.

4 Proverbs 22:6.

5 Genesis 2:18.

6 Genesis 1:28.

7 Romans 1:18.

8 See Sarah Blaffer Hrdy, *Mother Nature: Maternal Instincts and How They Shape the Human Species* (New York: Ballantine Books, 2000), 398–410.

9 Romans 10:4.

10 See Econ Househ, "The Evolution of Altruistic Preferences: Mothers versus Fathers," *US National Library of Medicine National Institutes of Health* 1, no. 11 (September 2013): 421–46. It may also be helpful to reference Alice Miller, *For Your Own Good: Hidden Cruelty in Child-Rearing and the Roots of Violence* (New York: Farrar, Straus, Giroux, 1983).

11 Paul D. Fairweather and Donovan D. Johnson, *Symbolic Regression Psychology* (New York: Irvington, 1981), 152.

12 Genesis 2:18.

13 Ephesians 5:31.

14 Genesis 2:23.

## Chapter 5

1 Fairweather, *Father Presence.*

2 1 Corinthians 12:14–20.

3 WA, TR, 5: 489, No. 6102.

4 See C. F. W. Walther and Walter C. Pieper, *God's No and God's Yes: The Proper Distinction between Law and Gospel* (St. Louis: Concordia, 1973).

5 Philip Melanchthon, BC, AC, VI, 40.

6 Luke 15:25–30.

7 Luke 15:31–32.

## Chapter 6

1 Romans 5:8.

2 Although no centralized text states Aquinas's doctrine of the *Analogia entis* directly and succinctly, the *Summa Theologiae*, 1a.13.1–6, covers the central issues. I typically reference Thomas Aquinas, Summa Theologiae: Latin Text and English Translation, Introductions, Notes, Appendices, and Glossaries (Cambridge, England: Blackfriars, 1964).

3 See C. G. Jung and R. F. C. Hull, *The Archetypes and the Collective Unconscious* (Princeton, NJ: Princeton University Press, 1980).

4 Edmund Fuller, *Myth, Allegory, and Gospel: An Interpretation of J. R. R. Tolkien, C. S. Lewis, G. K. Chesterton, Charles Williams* (Edmonton: Canadian Institute for Law, Theology, and Public Policy, 2000), 11–32.

5 Romans 1:18.

6 Bly, *Iron John*, x.

7 Rod Rosenbladt, "When Good Fathers Die, It's Always Too Early," podcast audio, n.d., https://shop.1517legacy.com/product/when-good-fathers-die-its-always-too-early-mp3.

8 See J. R. R. Tolkien, Verlyn Flieger, and Douglas A. Anderson, *Tolkien on Fairy-Stories* (London: HarperCollins, 2008).

9 Ibid., 71–72.

10 Roald Dahl and Patrick Benson, *The Minpins* (New York: Viking, 1991), 41.

11 Isaiah 25:6.

12 Revelation 19:7–9.

13 Mockingbird is a ministry that seeks to connect the Christian faith with the realities of everyday life in fresh and down-to-earth ways. Check them out at http://www.mbird.com/about/history-and-mission.

14 See AE, 45, *On the Estate of Marriage*. "Most certainly father and mother are apostles, bishops, and even priests to their children, for it is they who make them acquainted with the gospel. In short, there is not greater nobler authority on earth than that of parents over their children, for this authority is both spiritual and temporal. Whoever teaches the gospel to another is truly his apostle and bishop."

# Chapter 7

1 Genesis 2:22–25.

2 Ephesians 3:14–15.

3 G. K. Chesterton and Alvaro De Silva, *Brave New Family: G. K. Chesterton on Men and Women, Children, Sex, Divorce, Marriage and the Family* (San Francisco: Ignatius, 1990), 145.

4 See Pew Research Center, "Gender Gap in College Enrollment," accessed May 28, 2015, http://www.pewresearch.org/fact-tank/2014/03/06/womens-college-enrollment-gains-leave-men-behind.

5 This was originally written on March 16, 1955, as a letter to a "Mrs. Ashton" from Magdalene College, Oxford. Here is the quote in its entirety: "I think I can understand that feeling about a housewife's work being like that of Sisyphus (who was the stone rolling gentleman). But it is surely in reality the most important work in the world. What do ships, railways, miners, cars,

government etc. exist for except that people may be fed, warmed, and safe in their own homes? As Dr. Johnson said, 'To be happy at home is the end of all human endeavor'. (1st to be happy to prepare for being happy in our own real home hereafter: 2nd in the meantime to be happy in our houses.) We wage war in order to have peace, we work in order to have leisure, and we produce food in order to eat it. So your job is the one for which all others exist." C. S. Lewis, W. H. Lewis, and Walter Hooper, *Letters of C. S. Lewis* (San Diego: Harcourt, Brace, 1993), 447.

6  Chesterton and De Silva, *Brave New Family*, 143–44.

7  Martin Luther, BC, SC, 352.

8  Romans 13:9–10.

9  Fairweather and Johnson, *Symbolic Regression Psychology*, 152.

10  William H. Lazareth, *Luther on the Christian Home: An Application of the Social Ethics of the Reformation* (Literary Licensing, 2011), 138–53.

11  1 Corinthians 3:9.

12  WA, 10 III, 376. See also Lazareth, *Luther on the Christian Home*.

13  WA, 20, 149.

14  Fairweather and Johnson, *Symbolic Regression Psychology*, 152.

15  BC, SA IV, 319.

16  Martin Luther, BC, SA, Article 4, 319.

17  Psalm 127:1.

# Chapter 8

1  See Judith Warner, "'B.A.D.' Children, Worse Parents (and Even Worse Doctors)," in *We've Got Issues: Children and Parents in the Age of Medication* (New York: Riverhead Books, 2010).

2  1 Corinthians 1:18.

3  James A. Nestingen, "Preaching Repentance," *Lutheran Quarterly* 3 (1989): 249–65.

4  See NIH: National Institute of Mental Health, "Mental Illness Exacts Heavy Toll, Beginning in Youth," accessed May 29, 2015, http://www.nimh.nih.gov/news/science-news/2005/mental-illness-exacts-heavy-toll-beginning-in-youth.shtml.

5  Karl A. Menninger, *Whatever Became of Sin?* (Toronto: Bantam Books, 1988), 110.

6  Mary T. Clark Augustine, *Selected Writings* (New York: Paulist, 1984), 145.

7  Luke 15:24.

8  Luke 15:17.

9  Luke 15:18.

10  Luke 15:20–24.

## Chapter 9

    1  1 Corinthians 13:13.
    2  Luke 15:24 NIV.

## Chapter 10

    1  Luke 15:22–24.
    2  Psalm 103:13.
    3  Psalm 127:3–5.
    4  Exodus 20:12.
    5  Ephesians 6:1–4.
    6  1 Corinthians 13:1–13.
    7  Romans 10:4.
    8  See Romans 13:1–10.
    9  1 Thessalonians 2:11–12.
    10  Ephesians 5:23.
    11  Veith, *God at Work*, 161.
    12  George MacDonald, *A Hidden Life and Other Poems* (Eureka, CA: Sunrise Books, 1988), 3.
    13  Matthew 25:21.
    14  Luke 17:10.
    15  John 10:29.

# Bibliography

Augustine, Mary T. Clark. *Selected Writings*. New York: Paulist, 1984.

Bailey, Kenneth E. *The Cross and the Prodigal: A Commentary and Play on the Parable of the Prodigal Son*. St. Louis, MO: Concordia, 1973.

Bly, Robert. *Iron John: A Book about Men*. Cambridge, MA: Da Capo, 2004.

Capon, Robert Farrar. *The Parables of Grace*. Grand Rapids, MI: Wm. B. Eerdmans, 1988.

———. *The Parables of Judgment*. Grand Rapids, MI: Wm. B. Eerdmans, 1989.

———. *The Parables of the Kingdom*. Grand Rapids, MI: Wm. B. Eerdmans, 1989.

Chesterton, G. K., and Alvaro De Silva. *Brave New Family: G. K. Chesterton on Men and Women, Children, Sex, Divorce, Marriage and the Family*. San Francisco: Ignatius, 1990.

*Criminal Justice and Behavior* 14 (1978): 403–26.

Dahl, Roald, and Patrick Benson. *The Minpins*. New York: Viking, 1991.

Dodd, C. H. *The Parables of the Kingdom*. New York: Charles Scribner's Sons, 1961.

Eggebeen, David J. "Does Fatherhood Matter to Men?" *Journal of Marriage and Family*, no. 63 (May 2001): 381–93.

"Facts for Features: Unmarried and Single Americans Week: September 19–25, 2010." U.S. Census Bureau. Accessed May 25, 2015. https://www.census.gov/newsroom/releases/archives/facts_for_features_special_editions/cb10-ff18.html.

Fairweather, Paul D. *Father Presence: The Obscure Voice of Empathy*. Aliso Viejo, CA: Author, 1997.

Fairweather, Paul D., and Donovan D. Johnson. *Symbolic Regression Psychology*. New York: Irvington, 1981.

Fuller, Edmund. *Myth, Allegory, and Gospel: An Interpretation of J. R. R. Tolkien, C. S. Lewis, G. K. Chesterton, Charles Williams*. Edmonton: Canadian Institute for Law, Theology, and Public Policy, 2000.

*The Holy Bible: ESV (English Standard Version) Containing the Old and New Testaments*. Wheaton, IL: Crossway Bibles, 2008.

Househ, Econ. "The Evolution of Altruistic Preferences: Mothers versus Fathers." *US National Library of Medicine National Institutes of Health* 1, no. 11 (September 2013): 421–46.

Hrdy, Sarah Blaffer. *Mother Nature: Maternal Instincts and How They Shape the Human Species*. New York: Ballantine Books, 2000.

Jung, C. G., and R. F. C. Hull. *The Archetypes and the Collective Unconscious*. Princeton, NJ: Princeton University Press, 1980.

Koenig, Richard Edwin. *A Creative Minority: The Church in a New Age*. Minneapolis, MN: Augsburg, 1971.

Kolb, Robert, Timothy J. Wengert, and Charles P. Arand, ed. *The Book of Concord: The Confessions of the Evangelical Lutheran Church*. Minneapolis, MN: Fortress, 2000.

Laughlin, Lynda. "Who's Minding the Kids? Child Care Arrangements: Spring 2011." U.S. Census Bureau. Accessed May 28, 2015. https://www.census.gov/prod/2013pubs/p70-135.pdf.

Lazareth, William Henry. *Luther on the Christian Home: An Application of the Social Ethics of the Reformation*. Philadelphia: Muhlenberg Press, 1960.

Lewis, C. S. *The Four Loves*. New York: Harcourt, Brace, 1960.

Lewis, C. S., W. H. Lewis, and Walter Hooper. *Letters of C. S. Lewis*. San Diego: Harcourt, Brace, 1993.

Low, Robbie. "The Truth about Men and Church." *Touchstone: A Journal of Mere Christianity* 16, no. 5 (2003).

Luther, Martin. *Commentary on the Epistle to the Galatians*. Grand Rapids, MI: Zondervan, 1949.

———. *Luthers Werke auf CD-ROM: (Weimarer Ausgabe)*. Cambridge: Chadwyck-Healey, 2000.

MacDonald, George. *A Hidden Life and Other Poems*. Eureka, CA: Sunrise Books, 1988.

McLanahan, Sara, and Gary D. Sandefur. *Growing Up with a Single Parent: What Hurts, What Helps.* Cambridge, MA: Harvard University Press, 1994).

Meeker, Margaret J. *Strong Fathers, Strong Daughters: 10 Secrets Every Father Should Know.* New York: Ballantine Books, 2007.

Menninger, Karl A. *Whatever Became of Sin?* Toronto: Bantam Books, 1988.

Miller, Alice. *For Your Own Good: Hidden Cruelty in Child-Rearing and the Roots of Violence.* New York: Farrar, Straus, Giroux, 1983.

Mitscherlich, Alexander. *Society without the Father: A Contribution to Social Psychology.* New York: Harper Perennial, 1993.

Nestingen, James Arne. "Preaching Repentance." *Lutheran Quarterly* 3 (1989): 249–65.

Nestingen, James Arne, and Gerhard O. Forde. *Free to Be: A Handbook to Luther's Small Catechism.* Minneapolis, MN: Augsburg, 1975.

NIH: National Institute of Mental Health. "Mental Illness Exacts Heavy Toll, Beginning in Youth." Accessed May 29, 2015. http://www.nimh.nih.gov/news/science-news/2005/mental-illness-exacts-heavy-toll-beginning-in-youth.shtml.

Oden, Michael S. *When Nobody's Home: The Truth behind Drug and Alcohol Addiction through the Eyes of a Probation Officer.* Bloomington, IN: Author House, 2014.

Pew Research Center. "Gender Gap in College Enrollment." Accessed May 28, 2015. http://www.pewresearch.org/fact-tank/2014/03/06/womens-college-enrollment-gains-leave-men-behind.

Popenoe, David. *Life without Father: Compelling New Evidence That Fatherhood and Marriage Are Indispensable for the Good of Children and Society.* New York: Free Press, 1996.

Rosenblatt, Rod. "When Good Fathers Die, It's Always Too Soon." Podcast audio. n.d. https://shop.1517legacy.com/product/when-good-fathers-die-its-always-too-early-mp3.

Thielicke, Helmut. *The Waiting Father; Sermons on the Parables of Jesus.* New York: Harper, 1959.

Tolkien, J. R. R., Verlyn Flieger, and Douglas A. Anderson. *Tolkien on Fairy-Stories.* London: HarperCollins, 2008.

Veith, Gene Edward. *God at Work: Your Christian Vocation in All of Life.* Wheaton, IL: Crossway Books, 2002.

Walther, C. F. W., and Walter C. Pieper. *God's No and God's Yes: The Proper Distinction between Law and Gospel*. St. Louis, MO: Concordia, 1973.

Warner, Judith. *We've Got Issues: Children and Parents in the Age of Medication*. New York: Riverhead Books, 2010.

Wilson, Douglas. *Father Hunger: Why God Calls Men to Love and Lead Their Families*. Nashville, TN: Thomas Nelson, 2012.

Wingren, Gustaf. *The Living Word: A Theological Study of Preaching and the Church*. Philadelphia: Muhlenberg Press, 1960.

40493232R00094

Made in the USA
Middletown, DE
14 February 2017